Praying with the Saints by Season: Spring

PRAYING WITH THE SAINTS BY SEASON

SPRING

FR. PATRICK TROADEC, SSPX

Translated by Michael J. Miller
and Susan Treacy

PO Box 217 | Saint Marys, KS 66536

Original edition, *Prier un printemps avec les saints, au jour le jour* (Versailles: Via Romana, 2018)

Cover: *Passing Shower on a Spring Afternoon,* 1846, Francis Jasper Cropsey (1823-1900)

Library of Congress Control Number: 2022946450

© 2024 Angelus Press
All rights reserved.

ANGELUS PRESS
PO Box 217
Saint Marys, Kansas 66536
Phone (816) 753-3150
Fax (816) 753-3557
Order Line (800) 966-7337
www.angeluspress.org

ISBN: 978-1-68529-027-6
FIRST PRINTING—January 2024

Printed in the United States of America

Table of Contents

Note to the Reader _____ 1
The Saints Selected _____ 2

St. Joseph (Mar. 20) _____ 4
St. Benedict (Mar. 21) _____ 6
St. Leah (Mar. 22) _____ 8
St. Joseph Oriol (Mar. 23) _____ 10
St. Gabriel (Mar. 24) _____ 12
Annunciation of the Blessed Virgin (Mar. 25) ___ 14
Blessed Rizziero della Muccia (Mar. 26) _____ 17
St. John Damascene (Mar. 27) _____ 19
St. John of Capistrano (Mar. 28) _____ 21
Blessed Stephen X (Mar. 29) _____ 24
St. John Climacus (Mar. 30) _____ 27
St. Amos (Mar. 31) _____ 29
St. Hugh of Grenoble (Apr. 1) _____ 32
St. Francis of Paola (Apr. 2) _____ 34
St. Richard of Chichester (Apr. 3) _____ 37
St. Isidore of Seville (Apr. 4) _____ 39
St. Vincent Ferrer (Apr. 5) _____ 41
St. William of Eskill (Apr. 6) _____ 44
St. Maria Crescentia (Apr. 7) _____ 46
St. Walter of Pontoise (Apr. 8) _____ 48
St. Mary of Egypt (Apr. 9) _____ 50
St. Fulbert of Chartres (Apr. 10) _____ 52
St. Leo the Great (Apr. 11) _____ 54
St. Gemma Galgani (Apr. 12) _____ 57
St. Hermenegild (Apr. 13) _____ 59
St. Justin (Apr. 14) _____ 62
St. Peter González (Apr. 15) _____ 64

Praying with the Saints: Spring

St. Benedict-Joseph Labre (Apr. 16)	66
St. Louis-Marie de Montfort (Apr. 17) (celebrated on the 28th)	69
St. Marie of the Incarnation (Apr. 18)	72
St. Peter-Mary Chanel (Apr. 19) (celebrated on the 28th)	74
St. Agnes de Montepulciano (Apr. 20)	76
St. Anselm (Apr. 21)	79
Sts. Soter and Caïus (Apr. 22)	82
St. George (Apr. 23)	84
St. Fidelis of Sigmaringen (Apr. 24)	87
St. Mark (Apr. 25)	90
St. Zita (Apr. 26) (celebrated the 27th)	92
St. Peter Canisius (Apr. 27)	94
St. Paul of the Cross (Apr. 28)	97
St. Peter of Verona (Apr. 29)	100
St. Catherine of Siena (Apr. 30)	102
St. Marculf (May 1)	104
St. Athanasius (May 2)	106
Finding of the Holy Cross (May 3)	109
St. Monica (May 4)	112
St. Pius V (May 5)	114
St. Dominic Savio (May 6)	116
St. Stanislaus, Bishop (May 7)	118
The Apparition of Saint Michael (May 8)	120
St. Gregory of Nazianzus (May 9)	123
St. Solange (May 10)	126
St. Gengulphus (May 11)	128
St. Pancras (May 12)	131
St. Robert Bellarmine (May 13)	133
St. Pontius (of Cimiez) (May 14)	135
St. John Baptist de la Salle (May 15)	137
St. John Nepomucene (May 16)	140
St. Pascal Baylon (May 17)	142

Table of Contents

St. Felix of Cantalice (May 18) — 145
St. Yves (May 19) — 147
St. Bernardine of Siena (May 20) — 149
St. Gisela, Abbess of Chelles (May 21) — 151
St. Rita (May 22) — 154
St. Didier (May 23) — 156
St. Vincent of Lerins (May 24) — 159
St. Gregory VII (May 25) — 162
St. Philip Neri (May 26) — 165
St. Bede the Venerable (May 27) — 167
St. Germain of Paris (May 28) — 170
St. Mary Magdalene de Pazzi (May 29) — 172
St. Joan of Arc (May 30) — 174
Queenship of the Bl. Virgin Mary (May 31) — 177
St. Angela Merici (June 1) — 180
St. Blandina (June 2) — 182
St. Clothilde (June 3) — 185
St. Francis Caracciolo (June 4) — 188
St. Boniface (June 5) — 190
St. Norbert (June 6) — 193
Ugandan Martyrs (June 7)
   (celebrated on the 3rd) — 196
St. Medard (June 8) — 198
Blessed Anna-Maria Taïgi (June 9) — 200
St. Margaret of Scotland (June 10) — 203
St. Barnabas (June 11) — 206
St. John of San Facundo (June 12) — 208
St. Anthony of Padua (June 13) — 210
St. Basil the Great (June 14) — 212
St. Germaine (June 15) — 215
St. John Francis Regis (June 16) — 218
St. Gregory Barbarigo (June 17) — 220
St. Ephrem (June 18) — 222
St. Juliana Falconieri (June 19) — 224

St. Alban (June 20) (celebrated on the 22nd) __ 227
St. Aloysius of Gonzaga (June 21) _____ 230

Prayers
Spiritual Communion _____ 234
The Mysteries of the Rosary _____ 235
The Apostles' Creed _____ 236
An Act of Faith _____ 237
An Act of Hope _____ 237
An Act of Charity _____ 237
An Act of Contrition _____ 237
Memorare _____ 238
Litany of the Sacred Heart _____ 238
Litany of the Blessed Virgin _____ 240
Prayer to St. Michael the Archangel _____ 242
Prayer for Priests _____ 242
Psalm 50 (Miserere) _____ 243
Latin Prayers _____ 245
Anima Christi _____ 247

Bibliography _____ 249

Note to the Reader

Dear Reader,

Following the publication of the booklet of meditations entitled *Praying With the Saints by Season: Winter*, here is the second in the series, focusing on the lives of the saints commemorated by the Church in the spring. For each day a citation from Sacred Scripture is provided, followed by a summary of the life or the praises of the saint of the day.

Two thoughts, expressed by the saint himself or related to his life, help to foster meditation. In order for it to produce abundant, concrete, and lasting fruits, one or two prayers and three resolutions are also offered for each day. The whole presentation takes less than two pages.

So that the reader can recognize the saints when they visit churches or museums, the booklet often notes their attributes and emblems. It also describes their patronage and the circumstances in which they are customarily invoked.

Finally, in order to foster piety, while remaining in the spirit of the meditation, several prayers and canticles are added as an appendix to the volume.

St. Francis de Sales wrote: "What are the lives of the saints but the Gospel put into practice? There is no more difference between the written Gospel and the lives of the saints than there is between the *notes* for a piece of music and that same piece *sung*."[1] The saints are true artists, who interpret very correctly the inspired melodies that are *noted* in Sacred Scripture. Thus their lives appear like a prelude to the sounds of the eternal hymns sung in unison by the choirs of angels and the elect.

The saints lived in various eras, in very different situations, but they are close to us because of their attractiveness and are just waiting for our prayers in order to help us. Besides the better known saints, this booklet introduces

---

[1] Letter to Monseigneur André Frémyot, Archbishop of Bourges, dated 5 October 1604, *Oeuvres complètes*, vol. XII (Annecy: J. Niérat, 1902), 306.

many others who also deserve our admiration, veneration, and to a certain extent imitation.

While meditating on their lives attentively and with devotion, you will feel very small in comparison to them, but at the same time you will feel encouraged to become better, especially if you follow this valuable advice given by Monsignor Ghika: "The best way to celebrate the saints is to resemble them. Why not try to live as they did, if only for one day, *their* day, the day consecrated and blessed by the Church, when they are 'on duty' to help us?"[2]

Assuring you of my priestly prayers, especially during the celebration of the Holy Sacrifice of the Mass, I commend myself to yours and thank you very much in advance.

Father Patrick Troadec

The Saints Selected

Every day the Church commemorates a large number of saints listed in the Roman Martyrology. In most cases the one celebrated by the Universal Church (1962 Missal) was chosen. The other saints were selected from among the commemorations proper to certain localities or religious communities. When two important saints are celebrated on the same day, the life of the second one has been shifted to a feria close to his or her feast.

Like the other booklets in the series, this one presents saints from all the periods of Church history. Among the saints from the Renaissance to the contemporary period, some are well known, such as Louis-Marie Grignion de Montfort, Dominic Savio, Philip Neri, and Louis of Gonzaga, but others deserve to be, such as Blessed Rizziero (O.F.M.) and Anna-Maria Taïgi, or Saints Gangulphus, Marculf, Pontius, and William of Eskill [or Æbelholt].

Every day the Church commemorates the martyrs in

---

[2] Prince Vladimir Ghika, *Pensées pour la suite des jours* (Paris: Beauchesne, 1962), 172.

Note to the Reader

her liturgy to encourage the faithful to carry their cross and follow the Divine Master. Every century has its own martyrs. This volume describes the lives of martyrs from the early Christian centuries: several popes, a Father of the Church, an Evangelist, and a Virgin, but it also recounts the lives of Saints Stanislaus (†11th century), John Nepomucene (†14th century), Fidelis of Sigmaringen (†17th century), those of the martyrs of Uganda and of St. Peter Chanel (†19th century).

To the saints who died *in odio fidei* [victims of hatred for the faith], the Church joins an impressive array of virgins, confessors, and doctors. Among them, she honors the great popes Stephen X, Gregory VII, and Pius V, and the holy founders Benedict (Benedictines), Louis-Marie Grignion de Montfort (the Montfort Fathers and the Daughters of Wisdom), Paul of the Cross (Passionists), John Baptist de La Salle (Brothers of the Christian Schools), Philip Neri (Oratorians), and Norbert (Premonstratensians).

Some saints died in the flower of their youth (Gemma Galgani, Germaine, Joan of Arc, Louis of Gonzaga), others after a long life (Francis de Paul, Germain of Paris, Hugh, Paul of the Cross, Robert Bellarmine). They came from all social circles and from widely different nationalities. Many come from Italy (31 saints) and France (25). Others were originally Spain (7), Portugal, Great Britain (5), Germany (3), the Netherlands, Poland, and Palestine (4), Egypt (3), Asia Minor (modern-day Turkey), Tunisia, and Uganda.

Although many of the blessed showed signs of sanctity at a very early age (Dominic Savio, John Baptist de La Salle), others went through a period of lukewarmness (Anselm, Peter González, Anna-Maria Taïgi), or of sin (Mary of Egypt).

Thus, in the course of reading these pages, everyone will be able to discover a saint within reach.

St. Joseph

March 20

GOD SPEAKS TO US

And he came to dwell in a city called Nazareth.
—St. Matthew 2:23

MEDITATION

St. Joseph is the head of a family which is the sacred model of Catholic homes. And so today, let us contemplate him again, this time during his life in Nazareth.

St. Joseph teaches us how to sanctify our work. Indeed, in his everyday tasks, he does not lose the presence of God. Each of his strokes with the plane or the saw is an act of love. The spirit of prayer is the atmosphere that St. Joseph's soul breathes. He revels more each day in his union with God. Raised to this height, he can see the relative insignificance of the concrete realities of life here below. Of course, he loves Judea, the country of his fathers, Jerusalem the city of the Temple, Bethlehem the town of his ancestors; he loves his relatives, his neighbors, his friends, and much more his very gentle Spouse, and above all Jesus the Divine Child; but all these dear ties he loves only as much as the Good Lord permits. He is therefore ready to sacrifice them if the will of the Father demands it, because he analyzes all events of the present life with the eyes of faith.

Since he leads his whole family according to God's will, the result is great peace. Who could describe the intimate union, the grace, the holiness, the heavenly love that reigned in the home of Nazareth? Let us contemplate the Holy Family and strive to make ours similar to it. Let us defend in our homes the same piety, the same purity, the same charity. Our houses will then very quickly become vestibules of paradise.

Our enemies today are attacking the family. The family is strong because it is united. "And so," they say, "let us divide it by divorce." It is strong because it is pure; "Let us do all that we can to unleash passions everywhere." It is strong because of its charity; "Let us destroy charity by proclaiming the reign of selfishness." Let us be vigilant so as not to fall into these traps that are set for us.

St. Joseph also gives us a fine example by his methodical, regular, and constant work. He spares no effort and supports his family by the sweat of his brow. Here again, he teaches us that happiness here below does not reside in wealth, but in peace of mind, in union with God, and in labor that is sometimes hidden but always fruitful in God's sight.

Finally, God allowed the life of St. Joseph to be strewn with trials so that we might learn not to be discouraged by the difficulties of life.

Prayer

Help us, O Joseph, mirror of the most admirable fatherhood…be with us in our joyful hours and in our sad hours, in our works and in our rest.

—Pius XII

Thoughts

- Bear very patiently with the weaknesses of others, their bodily weaknesses and their character faults.
  —St. Benedict, *PPJ*,[3] February 19

- Why support yourself? Because in doing this, we fulfill the law of Jesus Christ: "Bear one another's burdens and so you shall fulfill the law of Christ" (Gal 6:2).
  —St. Vincent de Paul, *PPJ*, April 18

Resolutions

1 Recite an Act of Charity. (See Appendix.)

2 Live a little more in the presence of God, imitating St. Joseph.

3 Discreetly perform some service at home that will give pleasure to all the members of the family.

---

[3] Abbreviated sources are expanded for each saint in the bibliography at the back of this volume.

St. Benedict

March 21

GOD SPEAKS TO US

Go forth.

—Genesis 12:1

MEDITATION

St. Benedict (*ca.* 480-543)—by his life and by his rule—teaches us that, in order to become saints, we ought to follow the command given by God to Abraham: Go forth! Indeed, life on earth is a march, a pilgrimage, an ascent towards Heaven. During this peregrination, we can stop. Some people—and they are legion today—stop by seeking their happiness in the pleasure of the senses. St. Benedict triumphed over this first temptation. While he was leading a solitary life in Subiaco (Italy), he had to face a great temptation against purity. To tame his body, he threw himself into a thorn bush. The blood that he shed healed his soul forever. That was how he obeyed the interior voice that had said to him: Go forth!

In the course of life, another occasion to stop on the way of perfection is to seek happiness within. To avoid this snare, St. Benedict always obeyed God and urged his monks to take the path of obedience. Our will is not made for itself, but for the infinite. So, it must follow the exhortation of God, who says to it: Go forth! Obedience, according to Bossuet, is "the rampart of humility, the support of perseverance, the life of the spirit, and the sure death of self-love."[4]

In earthly life, a third temptation lies in complacency in our virtues. To those who are satisfied with their degree of union with God, and who think they can now rest, the good Lord says again: Go forth! That is to say, do not fall asleep, keep watch. Indeed, to preserve a life of intimate union with God, it is necessary to feed it with a continual renewal of fervor. This is why St. Benedict calls the application of his

---

[4] Bossuet, *Oeuvres oratoires*, vol. IV (1892), p. 541.

rule "a small beginning."

O great Saint Benedict, intercede for me with God so that I may overcome temptations against the virtue of purity, that I may generously obey my superiors, and that I may avoid complacency in my virtues.

Attributes and invocation

St. Benedict is depicted with his religious habit, and holding the Rule. Sometimes he holds a cup, which recalls the miracle during the attempt to poison him. He is invoked against bladder ailments, pleuralgia, spells, inflammation, and fever.

Prayer

Great Saint Benedict, father, guide, and support of all who humbly place their trust in thee, deign, I beg of thee, to take me under thy kind protection, so that by the excellence of thy merits, I may obtain pardon of my sins and the grace to avoid henceforth all that could displease my God.
—Prayer, *PS*, I, p. 30

Thoughts

- Lead a life which is pure, sober, benevolent.
 —St. Benedict, *PPJ*, February 1

- So that your obedience may be pleasing to God and sweet to men, do what you are ordered to do without fear, without delay/hesitation, without weakness, without complaining, and without refusing.
 —St. Benedict, *PPJ*, June 18

Resolutions

1 Examine your conscience to see whether you are really seeking spiritual progress, and make a specific resolution accordingly.

2 During temptations against the virtue of purity, say immediately: "O Mary, my good mother, protect me!"

3 Obey while following the advice of the second thought of the day.

St. Leah

March 22

God speaks to us

If thou wilt be perfect, go sell what thou hast, and give to the poor, and thou shalt have treasure in heaven: and come follow me.

—St. Matthew 19:21

Meditation

While many poor people find it difficult to be content with their lot and tend to envy the rich, we find throughout Church history persons from the upper classes who distributed their wealth to the poor and lived the rest of their days in abject poverty. This comes from the fact that the Catholic spirit is a spirit of detachment. When God wants to enter a soul, He invites her to detach herself from her possessions in order to attach herself to Him, for only a soul free from all hindrances can enjoy divine intimacy here below and deserve to receive the crown of glory in Heaven in accordance with the promise of Jesus. Leah († *ca.* 383), by her life, illustrated this course.

A great, cultured Roman lady, she left the world after the death of her husband. She gave her possessions to the poor and entered a sort of monastery in Rome along with St. Marcella, a wealthy widow who was also part of the Roman aristocracy. Leah became the superior; she had the heart of a mother for her sisters. She edified the whole community by her example. After having lived with abundance, she was content with little. She mortified her flesh, slept very little, prayed much, and studied Holy Scripture under the direction of St. Jerome. She sought as much as possible to disappear from the eyes of men so as to please her divine Spouse.

At the end of this life, God rewarded her well, as St. Jerome writes, who mentions, in contrast, the sad fate of the Consul Pretextatus, who died the same year. "For a little pain endured on earth, Leah enjoys a perfect peace in Heaven, where she has been received by the angels. She is in the bosom of Abraham, where, with the poor man Lazarus, she sees the rich man and the consul formerly covered with purple and now covered with confusion: they ask for a drop of water to refresh themselves, without being able to obtain it. He whom she once knew at the height of honors and dignities, he who triumphantly went up to the Capitol, is now reduced to misery and confined to a prison of darkness and despair from which he will never emerge. And our blessed Leah, who lived in a very small house, who was poor and who was deemed insane in the judgment of the world, is today received at the feast of the Lamb."[5]

O Saint Leah, you who passed voluntarily from riches to poverty, teach me to detach myself from the possessions of this world and to attach myself exclusively to spiritual goods, until I merit to join you one day in the blessed eternity of heaven.

Prayer

Hear our prayer, O God our Savior; grant that, in our joy in celebrating Saint Leah, we may also be animated by feelings of fervent piety. Through Jesus Christ. (Collect)

Thoughts

- Do not desire with envy what you do not have.
  —St. Benedict, *PPJ*, February 6

- Give everything on earth so as to recover everything in Heaven.
  —St. Benedict, *PPJ*, May 10

Resolutions

1 Meditate for ten minutes on the last things in order to have the courage to detach yourself from the goods of this world.

2 Avoid unnecessary expenses; do not hoard unnecessarily.

3 Donate to a good cause.

---

[5] *Letters of Saint Jerome,* in PL, v. XXII, col. 425.

St. Joseph Oriol
March 23

GOD SPEAKS TO US

Blessed is that servant, whom when his lord shall come, he shall find so doing. Amen, I say to you, he shall place him over all his goods.

—St. Matthew 24:46-47

MEDITATION

Joseph Oriol (1650-1702) was born in Barcelona (Spain). Since his father had died a little after Joseph's birth, his mother remarried a cobbler. This man took a liking to Joseph and entrusted his education to the chaplains of the Church of Mary, Star of the Sea. The boy was very receptive to instruction and already showed great piety. Joseph pursued his studies at the University of Barcelona. He took courses in literature, philosophy, and theology, and in 1674 became a doctor of theology. To help his poor mother, who had been widowed again, Joseph became a tutor to a rich family; there he led an exemplary life. In 1686 his mother died; he then left on foot for a pilgrimage to Rome. When he returned to Barcelona in June 1687, Joseph became parish priest of Santa Maria del Pino, a position he held for fifteen years, until his death.

He was above all a man of God; Joseph lived constantly in His presence. Joseph went to confession each day, then celebrated the Holy Sacrifice of the Mass with great devotion, prolonging afterwards his thanksgiving. He practiced exceptional mortification, sleeping only two hours a night on a bench. That did not lead him to have a sad or morose character; on the contrary, since the faithful nicknamed him "the joyful saint." He strove to love all men and took particular care of the sick. He gave all his income to the poor and used the inheritance that he had received on the death of his mother to have Masses celebrated on behalf of the deceased. While being very concerned about the salvation of his faithful, he nurtured the desire to go to Japan or to another mission land to convert unbelievers. He left Barcelona on April 2, 1696, but he was stopped in his tracks in Marseilles, where he fell gravely ill. He then retraced his steps. His faithful greeted him again with overflowing joy.

During the last part of his life, Joseph was almost continually in ecstasy. God permitted him to be tormented by the devil, but the saint resisted him firmly. He also received the gift of healing to the point of worrying the doctors and apothecaries. Each day around three o'clock, after the chanting of Vespers, the church of Santa Maria del Pino filled up with sick people. The saint laid his hands on them or made the sign of the cross over them with his thumb moistened with holy water. He also read hearts, which greatly facilitated the confessions of the faithful. He died of pleurisy, without agony, without effort, with a calm and smiling face, confident of receiving from Jesus the wages promised to a good and faithful servant.

Prayer

Hear, O Lord, the supplications that we address to Thee on the solemnity of Thy blessed Confessor Joseph, so that, placing no trust in our own virtue, we may be aided by the merits of him who pleased Thee. Through Jesus Christ. (Collect)

Thoughts

- The priesthood is the love of the heart of Jesus.
  —The Curé d'Ars, *PPJ*, June 29

- The priest is not for himself…He is not for himself; he is for you.
  —The Curé d'Ars, *PPJ*, October 19

Resolutions

1. Pray the First Joyful Mystery for the priests who supported us with their prayers and their example.
2. Examine your vocation before God.
3. Try to be joyful and smile in all circumstances; it is a beautiful witness which the world needs.

St. Gabriel

March 24

God speaks to us

Bless the Lord, all ye His angels: you that are mighty in strength, and execute His word, hearkening to the voice of His orders.

—Psalm 102:20

Meditation

God who has created us for heaven gives us all the graces needed to arrive there. He placed us in particular under the protection of innumerable armies of celestial spirits.

Today the Church celebrates one of them: St. Gabriel. According to the most likely belief, he is part of the choir of seraphim, the first choir of the celestial hierarchy. He himself declares that he is one "who stands before the throne of God (Lk. 1:19)." This title is the one also used by Raphael in speaking to Tobias (Tob.12:15). Now, it is recognized that St. Raphael is one of the most sublime angels of the choir of the seraphim.

Moreover, what confirms Gabriel's excellence is the mission to the Blessed Virgin that would be entrusted to him. As St. Gregory says, "to convey the most sublime message that ever was and ever will be, it was necessary to send the most sublime angel, or, at least, one of the most sublime."

St. Gabriel is above all an adorer of God, but the good Lord entrusted to him, besides, missions concerning the salvation of mankind. His name means "strength of God," the divine strength appears mainly in this humble mystery of the incarnation of the Word.

The great archangel announced to Daniel the time of the realization of the mystery of the Incarnation by the prophecy of the seventy weeks of years (Dan.9:24); he prophesied to Zachary the birth of St. John the Baptist, who was to prepare the way for Our Lord, and he asked Our Lady to agree to become the mother of the sweet Savior of mankind.

According to some Doctors, Gabriel was also the one

who appeared to the shepherds to announce the good news of the birth of Jesus, which would make them rejoice. Finally, according to the Dominican Breviary, when Our Lord fell in agony on the evening of Holy Thursday, it was St. Gabriel who came to strengthen Him.

O great Archangel Saint Gabriel, considering so many privileges which have been granted to you by God, my soul is filled with a holy respect for you. I turn to you today to implore your help. "Strength of God," come to my aid when my spiritual, psychological, or physical strength fails me.

Watch over me, protect me, defend me, pray for me! Assist me in the battle that I have to wage against the devil! Be my strength during my entire life and at the hour of my death, so that one day I can join my voice to yours to glorify God and His most holy Mother in the blessed eternity of heaven.

Prayer

O God, Who from among all the Angels didst choose the Archangel Gabriel to announce the mystery of Thine Incarnation: mercifully grant that we who keep his feast on earth may experience the effect of his patronage in heaven. Who livest and reignest. (Collect)

Thoughts

- May the angels of God cover you with their wings and guard you throughout the journey of life.
  —Élisabeth de la Trinité, *PPJ*, October 3

- The angels who are responsible for watching over us constantly present all our acts to the Lord, day and night.
  —St. Benedict, *PPJ*, October 2

Resolutions

1 Chant or recite a *Magnificat* to thank God for having sent his Son to redeem us. (See Appendix).

2 Turn off your cell phone to be more receptive to the inspirations of your guardian angel.

3 Answer your mail; send a consolation e-mail.

Annunciation of the Blessed Virgin

March 25

God speaks to us

Mary said to the angel: Behold the handmaid of the Lord; be it done to me according to thy word.

—St. Luke 1:38

Meditation

The austerity of Lent is suspended today to celebrate the great feast of the Annunciation. This solemnity brings to life again in the Church a moment in the history of humanity: the most Blessed Virgin Mary receives the visit of the archangel Gabriel, who asks her to become the Mother of God. She tells him: *I am the handmaid of the Lord.* A creature of God, I am on earth to accomplish His will. And so, I submit humbly to God's plan for me. How did she have the courage to say *yes* so promptly to the angel's request? It is because she learned to say *yes* to God from her earliest childhood.

At the very moment when she pronounced her *Fiat,* she received within her the Son of God, the Second Person of the Holy Trinity, the Word. God was made man, "the Word became flesh," the divine Heart began to beat. O prodigy of infinite Love! Why did Jesus Christ become incarnate? To redeem men from the sin of Adam and to open to them the gates of Heaven. The Incarnation of the Son of God was in view of their redemption. The three great mysteries of religion (the Trinity, the Incarnation, the Redemption) are brought together on this day.

Lord Jesus, I too, I want to be faithful in the little things of daily life. I know that my sanctification depends essentially on fidelity. "The one who is faithful in little things will also be so in great things (Lk. 16:10)." I will not forget this!

Annunciation of the Blessed Virgin

Prayer

The Son of the Father reposes in Mary, the Holy Ghost covers her with His shadow, her very pure womb has become heaven! Praise be to Thee, Most High, born of a Virgin; ineffable honor be to the Father, to the Son, and to the Holy Ghost. So be it. Amen.

—Hymn of St. Peter Damian

Thoughts

- Whatever trials the Lord may send you, whatever sacrifices He may ask of you, whatever duties He may impose on you, always have on your lips and in your heart this response of love and fidelity: "Behold Your servant."

  —St. Bernadette, *CNI*, p. 373

- When one is full of Jesus, one is full of charity…One hastens to do good because charity urges and does not want delay.

  —Charles de Foucauld, *NQ*, 1916

Resolutions

1. Pray your rosary well.
2. Give to your children some examples to allow them to imitate the *yes* of Mary: Yes, I strive to be attentive during my prayers…Yes, I form the habit of raising my soul to Jesus often for just a moment during my days…Yes, I apply myself to my class work…Yes, I hang my coat in its place as soon as I take it off…Yes, I set the table at the requested time and diligently…Yes, I make my bed every morning…Yes, I obey immediately…
3. As much as possible, attend the Mass of the Annunciation as a family.

SUGGESTIONS

- In families that are not accustomed to it, it would be excellent to highlight, at least once in a while, the prayer of the Angelus, on the occasion of the feasts of the Blessed Virgin, or on Saturday, a day which is especially dedicated to her. We can also begin to recite and meditate on the rosary regularly, at least a decade, if we do not yet do that.

- What does the Lord expect of me today? Consider, for example, going on a retreat in order to answer this question calmly.

Blessed Rizziero della Muccia

March 26

God speaks to us

And because thou wast acceptable to God, it was necessary that temptation should prove thee.

—Tobias 12:13

Meditation

Some worldly people may think that religious life is a life that flows like a calm river. In reality, all human beings here below must earn their Heaven. And so consecrated religious persons, even though they are effectively sheltered from many temptations, also have their trials. By God's permissive will, it can happen that some very fervent religious nevertheless go through periods of trouble, doubt, and even real interior storms. One of the most terrible temptations to endure concerns the mystery of predestination. Blessed Rizziero (†1236) had to face that.

Born in the Diocese of Camerino (Italy) to a noble and rich family, he was studying at the University of Bologna when one Assumption Day he attended a sermon given by St. Francis of Assisi. Captivated, he decided to abandon all to marry "Lady Poverty." A faithful disciple of St. Francis, he excelled in all the virtues so well that he was soon promoted to provincial minister of The Marches. He took great care to make sure that the friars observed the Rule perfectly, above all in matters concerned with poverty.

But then one day the thought occurred to Rizziero that St. Francis had foreseen his damnation and, consequently, Rizziero was convinced that the saint no longer loved him and that Francis was no longer praying for him. To overcome this terrible trial, Rizziero turned to prayer, to fasting, and to various sacrifices, but without result. And so, one day when the temptation was longer and more overwhelming, the exhausted Rizziero decided to make the journey to Assisi in order to consult with St. Francis and find out whether he was well disposed towards him. If St. Francis told Rizziero that he still held him in high regard, he would see it as a sign that he had been tempted by the devil.

St. Francis, having been warned by God about the trials endured by Rizziero, sent two of his disciples to tell him on the way: "Of all the friars, you are one of those whom Francis loves the most." This message sufficed to dispel the holy friar's anguish. Upon Rizziero's arrival in Assisi, St. Francis honored and reassured him and said to him: "God permitted this temptation to increase your merits; but if it is too heavy a burden for you, be delivered from it." In fact, the temptation disappeared once and for all.

A little later, Blessed Rizziero was present at the death of St. Francis, and he lived for another ten years in the most profound peace, edifying his neighbor by his virtues and miracles.

Prayer

O God, Who dost gladden us by the annual solemnity of Blessed Rizziero, Thy Confessor, deign that, celebrating his birth into heaven, we may imitate also the example of his life. Through Jesus Christ. (Collect)

Thoughts

- God, who is faithful, will not suffer you to be tempted above that which you are able.

    —I Corinthians 10:13

- One single act of love made during a period of spiritual dryness is worth more than a hundred made during a period of consolations.

    —Padre Pio, *PPJ*, October 7

Resolutions

1. Pray and meditate for ten minutes the Act of Hope (See Appendix).

2. Say a prayer or offer a sacrifice for a desperate soul.

3. Have immediate recourse to God in temptations.

St. John Damascene

March 27

God speaks to us

Thou hast held me by my right hand, and by Thy will Thou hast conducted me, and with Thy glory Thou hast received me.
—Introit: Psalm 72:24

Meditation

John Damascene (676-749) was born in Damascus, Syria, under Muslim rule. While his father, a Greek Catholic, filled the role of minister of the caliph, his tutor was an Italian monk held captive by the Saracens. He eagerly received religious instruction and grew at the same time in the practice of the virtues.

At the death of his father, he was called to succeed him in the office of minister of the caliph, and soon as governor of Damascus.

During this period, some events drew attention to John. In 726, Leo III the Syrian, Emperor of Constantinople, forbade devotion to holy images, and four years later, he ordered their destruction. St. John ardently opposed this measure, which was contrary to all tradition. To take revenge, the Emperor devised a scheme to tarnish the saint's reputation with the caliph. The latter, credulous, fell into the trap, and ordered that John's right hand be cut off. After the amputation, moved by a great confidence in Our Lady, John made an ardent prayer to the Blessed Virgin who, during his sleep, restored his severed hand.

A little after, he entered the monastery of St. Sabbas near Jerusalem. He was welcomed there by an old man with a grumpy temperament; John endured the worst humiliations with the utmost patience. He was forbidden all secular study and writing. He submitted without flinching to these harsh prohibitions.

After such a rigorous novitiate, he again received permission to study, to his very great joy. He proved to be a poet through his writings, notably in the hymns that he composed, but he was above all the author of a theological trilogy, the *Source of Knowledge*, of a book of heresies, and of a treatise on the orthodox faith. He also laid the foundations of Marian theology. He was nicknamed by the Byzantines: Chrysorroas, "he who causes gold to flow."

Saint John, model of patience, support me. Pray to God to help me not to rebel in times of trial, and to maintain serenity and trust in Providence.

Attributes

St. John Damascene is depicted as a Doctor of the Church, with a book, and holding his severed hand.

Prayer

O Almighty and everlasting God, Who didst fill blessed John with heavenly learning and with wonderful fortitude of spirit, that he might uphold the devotion due to holy images: grant us through his intercession and example, that we who revere the images of the saints may both imitate their virtues and enjoy their patronage. Through Our Lord. (Collect)

Thoughts

- What a book is to those who know how to read, a picture is to those who do not; what the word is to hearing, the image is to sight. The holy images are a memorial of divine works.
  —St. John Damascene
- Silence is the mother of prayer, and prayer is the manifestation of divine glory.
  —St. John Damascene, *PG*, 96, 561ab

Resolutions

1 Meditate for ten minutes on the life of St. John Damascene.

2 Imitate one of the virtues of this saint: his piety, humility, strength, and Marian devotion.

3 Have in your house beautiful paintings and crucifixes, beautiful images, or statues to nourish your piety.

St. John of Capistrano

March 28

God speaks to us

I have fought a good fight, I have finished my course, I have kept the faith. As to the rest, there is laid up for me a crown of justice.

—II Timothy 4:7-8

Meditation

John (1386-1456) was born in Capistrano, in the Abruzzi (Italy). He studied the liberal arts and law, then he became governor of the city of Perugia, which he defended against the lords of Rimini. Betrayed and thrown in prison, he tried vainly to escape. He benefited then from an apparition of St. Francis of Assisi, who consoled him. And so he decided a little later to enter the Franciscan order (1415). For his theology instructor he had St. Bernardine of Siena (†1444), who transmitted to him his devotion to the sweet names of Jesus and Mary.

Ordained a priest in 1417, he began his mission as an itinerant preacher, which lasted for forty years. He preached at least once a day. He had the people pile up their frivolous paintings, playing cards, and trinkets of feminine coquetry on the town squares, and then set them on fire. Crowds knelt at his feet in the confessional. In Rome, he converted the leader of a synagogue and about forty other Jews after an oratorical contest. Among the Hussites he prompted more than twelve thousand conversions, even among the nobility.

His activity as a religious superior (econome then vicar general) and legislator of the Observants was important. He sought to restore fervor to the whole Franciscan order and attracted around four thousand candidates to the religious life. As inquisitor, he successfully struggled against the influence of the *Fraticelli* (or Spiritual Franciscans), errant Franciscans who had rejected all the popes for the last eighty years and rejected the idea that the Church should own anything.

John was the personal counselor to three popes. In 1451, Frederick III, Emperor of Germany, made an appeal to the Pope to avert the Muslim invasion. Thus Calixtus III proclaimed the crusade against the Turks. From 1454 on, John took part in it. In 1456, the Pope sent him to John Hunyadi, who was defending Belgrade against the Sultan Mahomet II. John of Capistrano fired up the troops, and they won the victory on July 14. One hundred twenty thousand Muslims were slain or put to flight. "By virtue of my name and of the Holy Cross, you will win the victory over the Turks," Jesus had predicted to him. After the battle, thousands of corpses were rotting around the city, resulting in an epidemic of the black plague which caused the death of the holy Franciscan on October 23, after he had pronounced the sweet name of Jesus.

Prayer

Illustrious soldier of Jesus Christ, O John, you gained immortal fame by your word and by your works. By the Cross, you put the Turks to flight, by the Cross, you dispelled diseases; you helped by the Cross all those of whom you were the leader. Implore for us forgiveness of our faults, along with constancy in the faith and fidelity to the law of this Jesus whom you loved so much.
—Hymn to St. John of Capistrano, *Au. S.*, IV, p. 194

Thoughts

- For me, though overwhelmed with old age, I resolved to lay down my life and give my blood for the honor of the name of Christ and the preservation of the faith.
    —St. John of Capistrano, *Au. S.*, IV, p. 174

- Do not be afraid; we are defending the cause of God and the name of Christ; I am certain that God will make His cause triumph.
    —St. John of Capistrano, *Au. S.*, IV, p. 188

Resolutions

1 Recite the First Sorrowful Mystery, praying to Our Lady to convert a Muslim acquaintance.
2 Confess your faith, for example, by hanging a rosary from your rear view mirror.
3 Be modest in your dress.

Blessed Stephen X

March 29

GOD SPEAKS TO US

Lo, I have set thee this day over the nations, and over the kingdoms, to root up, and pull down, and to waste, and to destroy, and to build, and to plant, says the Lord.

—Offertory: Jeremias 1:10

MEDITATION

Frederick, son of Gozelon, Duke of Lorraine, was the maternal grandson of Bérenger II, last king of Italy. He was promoted canon archdeacon of Saint-Lambert Cathedral in Liège, where he was trained. In 1051, having been appointed Chancellor of the Roman Church by Pope Leo IX, he went to Constantinople and called on Michael I Cerularius to try to unite the Greek Church with the Latin Church. Unfortunately, the attempt failed. A little later, the Pope died. Frederick decided then to retire as a monk to Monte Cassino. Abbot Richer received him, but he died in turn. Frederick was chosen to replace him. Pope Victor II, happy with this decision, created Frederick cardinal-priest with the title of St. Chrysogonus, and one week later, granted him the abbatial blessing. But the new pope also died. On August 2, 1057, Frederick was chosen by acclamation to succeed him. He received the name of Stephen. He was consecrated the next day, in the presence of the cardinals, the clergy, and a crowd of the faithful.

During his short pontificate, Stephen substituted the Roman chant for Ambrosian chant. He tried to restore peace in the Church of Milan, created St. Peter Damian Cardinal of Ostia, and above all, he held synods to combat the incontinence of clerics. During the time of his reign in Rome, the Church was in the throes of great moral decadence. And so Stephen expelled from the clergy those who, since the prohibition by Pope Leo IX, had lived in incontinence, forbidding them to celebrate Mass in the future unless they had left their wives and embraced penance. This measure was based both on the unanimous affirmation of the Fathers of the Church and on that of the Apostles who had been married before Christ called them, then ceased married life and practiced perfect continence. This living rule constituted by the example of the Apostles largely contributed to the establishment of the discipline of priestly celibacy from the beginning of the Church. There is a canonical prescription on this subject in 390, in Carthage. Unfortunately, over the centuries there have been periods of decline, but the Church has always reacted against abuses by taking serious measures, like that of Blessed Stephen. The saintly pope died after about ten months of his pontificate, assisted at his deathbed by Hugh, abbot of Cluny.

Prayer

Eternal shepherd, consider with benevolence your flock and guard them with perpetual protection by your blessed Supreme Pontiff Stephen, whom you appointed pastor of the entire Church. Through Jesus Christ, our Lord. (Collect)

Thoughts

- A priest ought to be adorned with all the virtues and give to others the example of a pure life. His morals should not resemble those of the people: he should not walk in the common ways; but he must live like the angels in Heaven or like perfect men on earth.
    —*The Imitation of Christ,* Book IV, chap. 5

- I am, said Jesus, the friend of purity, and from Me all holiness comes. I seek a pure heart, and that is the place of My rest.
    —*The Imitation of Christ,* Book IV, ch. 12

RESOLUTIONS

1 Pray the Fifth Sorrowful Mystery to implore the amendment of unfaithful priests.
2 Pray a *Memorare* that the Pope will have the courage to remind people of the Catholic doctrine on marriage.
3 Avoid any inappropriate attitude in the presence of a priest, remembering his sublime vocation.

St. John Climacus

March 30

God speaks to us

Blessed are they that mourn: for they shall be comforted.
—St. Matthew 5:5

Meditation

At the age of sixteen, John (*ca*. 575-*ca*. 650) presented himself on Mount Sinai to an old man named Martyr to do an apprenticeship in the solitary life. He received spiritual formation for four years, then publicly pronounced his profession to the religious life. For nineteen years, he practiced obedience with great simplicity. Upon the death of Martyr, John embraced the life of the anchorites. On Saturdays and Sundays he went to the church dedicated to the Blessed Virgin, where he met the other solitaries. He passed the rest of the week in prayer and manual labor and ate very little. He then overcame terrible temptations. In return, God gave him the gift of prayer and that of tears. According to him, "those who have received this gift [of tears] pass all the days of their lives in continual celebration; their sorrow contains inconceivable consolation and joy, as wax contains honey."[6] Having become a master of the spiritual life, he agreed to accept a disciple, a certain Moses. An abbot at a nearby monastery then asked John to write down the thoughts that the Holy Ghost dictated to him on the practice of the virtues. Using the image of Jacob's ladder, St. John described thirty steps to climb to reach salvation. Ladder is *"climax"* in Greek, thus the name Climacus was given to the saint.

To unite oneself with God, it is first a question of breaking with the world, then of practicing fundamental virtues such as obedience and penance while being mindful of death; the goal is to achieve simplicity, humility, and discernment. To this ascetic work it was necessary to join the struggle against thoughts of malice and against their

---

[6] *Histoires choisies des Pères des deserts d'Orient*, pp. 236-237.

satellites. Here the saint dealt with anger, spiritual laziness (*acedia*), gluttony, lust, avarice, and finally insensitivity and pride. The fight against his faults must be carried out in a common life before any apprenticeship in a solitary life, specified the saint. As the life of union with God increases in him, the mystic—like a mother who holds her beloved child in her arms—is drawn into the charity of God. St. John completed this beautiful teaching in his *Letter to the Pastor*.

After having governed for some time the monastery of Sinai, St. John returned to his solitude. He eventually appointed a successor named George, then gave his soul back to God.

Saint John, pray to God to help me to be detached from the spirit of the world and to practice the virtues of humility and charity, which will enable me to reach the happiness of heaven.

Prayer

I approach [You], Jesus, source of life and holiness, with the ardent desire to drink from this inexhaustible source.

—Father Gabriel, ID, I, p. 25

Thoughts

- Life is a ladder by which Jesus delights to let souls climb.

    —St. Bernadette, *PPJ*, July 25

- To be a Christian is to imitate Christ as far as human beings can.

    —St. John Climacus, *The Ladder*, I, 633b

Resolutions

1 Find a quarter of an hour in the day in which to live closer to the good Lord while thinking of all He has done for you.

2 Fight particularly against a fault mentioned in the meditation above. Specify which one.

3 Be silent in adversity and to offer it to God.

St. Amos

March 31

God speaks to us

For thus saith the Lord to the house of Israel: Seek ye Me, and you shall live.

—Amos 5:4

Meditation

Amos was one of the twelve minor prophets of the Old Testament. He prophesied under Ozias of Judah (809-758 B.C.), and under Jeroboam II of Israel (825-784). He must have preceded Osee for some time, and followed Joel, under whose influence he came. His mission seems to have been of short duration. Nothing had prepared Amos to fulfill the role of prophet. He was a simple shepherd of Thecua, a small village south of Bethlehem. Nevertheless, he was far from being a peasant. Reading his writings, we perceive that he knew the Mosaic Law, that he was familiar with the Sacred Scriptures, that he had a certain ease in his manner of expressing himself as much by writing as by speaking. St. Augustine himself praised Amos' eloquence. Indeed, he had a style that was clear, limpid, and vigorous. He did not hesitate to use strong images alluding to nature and the pastoral life to interest his readers and his audience.

He went to Bethel, where King Jeroboam I had established the religion of the golden calf and he preached there that the vengeance of God would especially affect Israel on account of her idolatry. Israel would see her towns destroyed, her lands ravaged, her inhabitants sent into captivity. The neighboring peoples: the Syrians, the Philistines, the Idumeans, the Moabites, and the Ammonites would be affected. Even Judah would be punished because of her infidelity to the law. Calamities would rain down on all these lands because of their idolatry and moral corruption.

Happily, the prophecy ended on a note of hope. God would raise up again the house of David. Although it is true that the house of Israel would not be re-established, nevertheless it too would be called to enjoy the happiness of the Messianic kingdom. A priest of Bethel informed King Jeroboam II that the people were troubled by the predictions of Amos. As the king did not heed this warning, he himself went to see Amos to ask him to retire. The prophet told the priest Amasias what misfortunes would befall him. The prophet subsequently suffered the revenge of one of the sons of Amasias who struck him with a club, leaving him half dead. Amos was then transported to Thecua, where he died soon after.

Prayer

Let us bow before the avenging wrath, let us weep before the Judge; let us cry out with words of supplication, let us all speak, falling prostrate: Spare, O Lord, spare thy people: let not thy wrath be kindled against us forever.

—Chant: *Parce Domine*

Thoughts

- The Lord God hath sworn by his own soul, saith the Lord the God of hosts: I detest the pride of Jacob, and I hate his houses, and I will deliver up the city with the inhabitants thereof…Jeroboam shall die by the sword, and Israel shall be carried away captive out of their own land.

  —Amos 6:8, 7:11

- And I will bring back the captivity of my people Israel: and they shall build the abandoned cities, and inhabit them: and they shall plant vineyards, and drink the wine of them: and shall make gardens, and eat the fruits of them.

  —Amos 9:14

Resolutions

1 Recite three times the excerpt from *Parce Domine* (above) so that Christians in our country may once again be faithful to the promises of their baptism.

2 Make known the warnings given by the Blessed Virgin in her apparitions to enlighten your neighbor about the danger that evils will rain down on our country if it does not convert.

3 Read in the Bible the prophecy of Amos.

St. Hugh of Grenoble

April 1

GOD SPEAKS TO US

Behold a great priest who, in his days, pleased God.
—Gradual: Ecclesiasticus 44:16

MEDITATION

While in the world men greedily seek power, saints shun honors. Only when they have certain signs from Divine Providence do they accept honorary positions. They know indeed that, according to the adage: *honor, onus*, honor is a burden. The superior will have to answer before God for the salvation of the souls entrusted to him. Hugh (1053-1132) understood this well; hence the reservations that he expressed before receiving the episcopate.

He was born near Valence, in the Dauphiné (France). As she carried him in her womb, his mother saw him in a dream in the form of a child whom St. Peter was leading to Heaven in the company of other saints: what a happy omen! While still young, Hugh held the office of canon in the cathedral church of Valence; then he was named Bishop of Grenoble. Consecrated a bishop by the Pope at the age of twenty-seven, he attacked the evils that Stephen X (see March 29) had fought against in Italy: simony (ecclesiastical offices acquired, not by virtue of merits, but at a monetary price) and the immorality of priests. He resorted to all means to remedy it. In addition to his remonstrances and threats, he prayed, fasted, and gave alms. After two years of effort, not seeing any of the hoped-for results, he retired to the monastery of La Chaise-Dieu. He remained there one year, but, when Pope Gregory VII learned of this, he asked him to resume his post. The prelate submitted humbly to the injunction of the Supreme Pontiff. Three years later, he received a visit from St. Bruno, accompanied by six other monks, who asked him to authorize the foundation of a monastery. He had seen in a dream, a little time before, a building founded at la Chartreuse, and over it seven stars shining with a mysterious light. Seeing these pious men, he made the connection with the apparition and personally led them to the place designated by God. Afterwards, he liked to retire there regularly. His mortifications caused him a heaviness in the stomach and incessant headaches, but far from allowing himself to be overwhelmed by the discomfort that his illnesses caused, he found there an opportunity to intensify his life of union with God and his compassion towards his neighbor. An upright man, he had a sense of justice. His love for the poor led him to divest himself of his episcopal ring and of his chalice to help them. His preaching touched the hearts of his listeners. He thus passed easily from the pulpit to the confessional. Finally, he died at an advanced age, his soul loaded with merits.

Prayer

May the venerable intercession of blessed Abbot Hugh, we beg You, make us agreeable to Your Majesty; so that we who continually offend You may be purified by his continual prayers. Through Our Lord Jesus Christ. (Collect)

Thoughts

- Imitate the Lord, who said: "I have not come to do my will, but the will of Him who sent me.

    —St. Benedict, *PPF*, April 1

- Lust alone and vanity alone are capable of ruining us without the mercy of God.

    —St. Hugh

Resolutions

1 Pray the Third Joyful Mystery to ask Our Lady to deliver you from any form of greed.
2 Start your day with the most demanding work so as to accomplish God's will and not your own.
3 Search for moments of silence during the day to lift your spirit to God.

St. Francis of Paola

April 2

God speaks to us

Every one that exalteth himself shall be humbled, and he that humbleth himself shall be exalted.

—St. Luke 14:11

Meditation

Francis of Paola (1416-1508), born in Calabria (Italy), was endowed with great natural qualities. He shone, above all, by his humility. He had only one desire: to withdraw forever to a desert, to apply St. Bernard's motto: "love to be misunderstood." The good Lord had other plans for him. When he had barely reached his twentieth year, crowds flocked to Francis to find light and comfort; he preached humility to them. Soon, at the inspiration of the Holy Spirit, he founded the Order of Minims (Reformed Franciscans), giving it the same virtue as its foundation. He was named counselor to King Louis XI; if he went to the court, it was not because he enjoyed it, but only out of duty. It took the intervention of the Pope—in person—to persuade him to accept this mission. He entered the court only by the door of humility; he remained there undefiled, thanks to this virtue, and he would go out with it. He could claim some dignity in recompense for his zeal, but he did not want that.

Through humility, Francis refused the priesthood and even the diaconate. He remained a subdeacon his whole life. He was enriched by God with the gift of knowledge. Francis penetrated the secrets of hearts, saw what was happening on the other side of the world, announced the future. He predicted the fall of the Byzantine Empire if it persisted in schism, and the capture of Constantinople. He foretold to the King of Naples his victory over the Turks. He predicted to Ferdinand, King of Spain, that he would succeed in driving the Moors from his states. Francis also had the gift of miracles. One day, in the sight of a large crowd, he crossed the strait of Sicily by walking on the water. Another time, he carried an enormous rock to help in the construction of the first church that he built. At his voice an epidemic ceased immediately. Thus he seemed to dominate all the elements of nature.

After that, was it any wonder that all the powers of the earth honored Francis? Popes Paul II and Sixtus IV held him in high esteem; the French kings Louis XI and Charles VIII showed him the greatest veneration. Louis XI, who had a very difficult character and was feared even by his own entourage, became respectful and submissive in his sight. It was thanks to Francis, in great measure, that a happy union could be established between Charles VIII and Anne of Brittany, permitting the unification of Brittany with France. He died on a Friday at three o'clock, at the convent of Plessis-lès-Tours.

Attributes

St. Francis is depicted as a hermit with a long beard. His motto *humilitas* or *caritas* is surrounded by rays.

Prayer

O God, the exaltation of the lowly, Who hast raised Thy blessed Confessor Francis to the glory of the saints, grant, we beseech Thee, that by his merits and example we may happily obtain the rewards promised to the lowly. Through Our Lord. (Collect)

Thoughts

- God casts a preferential look on a soul who continually mistrusts herself, so that she recognizes sincerely that she has nothing to do with the good that is done in her or by her.

  —St. Bernadette, *PPJ*, September 16

- Why is Jesus so small in me? It is because I am not small enough, not humble enough. May I then become humble at last; let me humble myself, and Jesus will grow.

  —St. Bernadette, *PPJ*, December 30

RESOLUTIONS

1 Recite the Litany of Humility. (See Appendix.)
2 Avoid striving to be seen by others.
3 Accept unpleasant remarks without making excuses.

St. Richard of Chichester

April 3

GOD SPEAKS TO US

He glorified him in the sight of kings ... and shewed him His glory.

—Ecclesiasticus 45:3

MEDITATION

The life of Richard of Chichester (1197-1253), like that of all the saints, is interwoven with trials. He was born in England. His parents fell into profound material misery, his elder brother tried to remedy the situation, but failing to do so, he was thrown into prison. Richard then struggled to free his brother by assigning his own property to him. In this way the future bishop already showed his detachment from the goods of this world. One of his main interests then was study. He went to the University of Oxford, then to Paris. In the latter city he shared a room with two other students. They were so poor that they had to content themselves with one cloak for all three. Nevertheless, Richard later recalled that those were the most beautiful years of his life.

Subsequently he returned to England to teach humanities before going to Bologna to study law in greater depth. Seven years later he returned to Oxford, where he was particularly esteemed for his gentleness, modesty, chastity, and devotion. He was then elected chancellor of the university before withdrawing to the Dominicans of Orléans to study theology and receive priestly ordination. Upon his return to England, he administered a small parish in the diocese of Canterbury under the direction of St. Edmund.

In 1244, the Archbishop of Canterbury appointed him to succeed the Bishop of Chichester, but he had to fight to keep this position because of fierce opposition from Henry III. The showdown between the bishop and the king lasted for two years. Happily, Richard's right was upheld by Pope Innocent IV. The king, overcome by the threats of the pope, ended up leaving Richard to govern his diocese peaceably, and he restored to him the ecclesiastical goods of which he had been unjustly deprived. Richard, notably, showed a great solicitude for the pour. To those who were indignant at his conduct, he replied: "It is better to sell one's horse and one's silver dishes than to let the poor, who are members of Jesus Christ, suffer." God repaid his generosity through miracles. One day he fed three thousand paupers, and with what was left he could still nourish one hundred more. He also took an interest in the good of the universal Church by preaching in all of England the crusade to recover the holy places.

He died kissing the crucifix and invoking our good Heavenly Mother.

Prayer

Grant, O Almighty God, that the holy solemnity of blessed Richard, your confessor and bishop, may increase in us devotion and salvation. Through Jesus Christ Our Lord. (Collect)

Thoughts

- We ought to bless God in all the events of life.
  —Pauline Jaricot, *PPJ*, September 3

- Mary, Mother of God and of Mercy, defend us from the enemy and receive us at the hour of death.
  —St. Richard

Resolutions

1 Pray the Fifth Joyful Mystery for God to raise up holy bishops of the caliber of St. Richard for the greatest good of the Church.

2 Persevere in the struggle against your dominant fault.

3 Make a donation to a poor person or to a good work according to your means, with discernment (reflect upon to whom you give, how much, in what way).

St. Isidore of Seville

April 4

God speaks to us

For if it shall please the great Lord, he will fill him with the spirit of understanding…He shall shew forth the discipline he hath learned.

—Epistle: Ecclesiasticus 39:8, 11

Meditation

The purpose of marriage is to populate Heaven with the elect. What joy, then, for Severianus and Theodora to see their four children proclaimed saints in the sight of the world: Leander, Bishop of Seville (Spain), Isidore (†636), his successor in the episcopal see, Fulgentius, Bishop of Cartagena, and Florentina, a consecrated virgin. Three holy bishops and a nun: these are the splendid fruits of a profoundly Catholic household. Unfortunately, Isidore could not profit for very long from the wise counsels of his parents, for they died shortly after his birth. He was then placed under the guardianship of Leander— who was not gentle with him! Leander was very strict, but his firmness bore fruits: Isidore became the greatest scholar of his century and even the universal scholar of the Middle Ages. Yet he did not seek to shine in the world's sight. A lover of truth, he placed his knowledge at the service of the Church. He worked ardently for the conversion of the Arian Goths, the Jews, and also the Acephali, heretics who denied that Christ has two natures, divine and human.

At the death of his brother, Isidore succeeded him as head of the diocese for a duration of forty years. He defended law and justice, and strove to give young people a solid intellectual formation. He was present at the Second Council of Seville (618) and presided at the Fourth Council of Toledo (633). He wished that the liturgy be celebrated with majesty and devotion. He was at the origin of the Mozarabic rite. As bishop, he pursued erudite works, writing a dictionary of synonyms, a treatise on astronomy and geography, biographies of men of his century, of Old and New

Testament personages, and the history of the Goths with their conquests and rule, and an encyclopedia of etymologies…which earned him the title of Doctor of the Church. Isidore died at an advanced age.

"When on earth, thy vigilance over the flock entrusted to thy care was untiring; consider us as a part of it, and defend us from the ravenous wolves that cease not to seek our destruction."[7]

Attributes and patronage

St. Isidore is depicted as a bishop. He is the patron saint of Seville and of Leon.

Prayer

O God, who didst give blessed Isidore to Thy people as a minister of eternal salvation: grant, we beseech Thee, that we, who have had him for our teacher on earth, may deserve to have him for our advocate in heaven. Through Our Lord. (Collect)

Thoughts

- He is happy who is wise according to God: the happy life is the knowledge of divinity and this is the fruit of good works.

    —St. Isidore

- We cannot always feel happy, but can always be happy if our will is united with God's.

    —St. Peter-Julian Eymard, *PPJ*, July 6

Resolutions

1. Pray the First Glorious Mystery for the members of your family while imploring perseverance in the faith for each one.
2. Give thanks to God for all the benefits received from Him so as to live joyfully.
3. Show good humor within your family.

---

[7] Dom Guéranger, *The Liturgical Year, Paschal Time*, II, tr. Dom Laurence Shepherd, OSB (Great Falls, Montana, 2000), p. 284.

St. Vincent Ferrer

April 5

GOD SPEAKS TO US

How beautiful are the feet of them that preach the gospel of peace, of them that bring glad tidings of good things!
—Romans 10:15

MEDITATION

Vincent Ferrer (1350-1419) was born in Valencia (Spain). Very gifted intellectually, he entered the Dominican convent at the age of seventeen. He pursued studies in Barcelona, Lerida, and Toulouse, then became a professor of philosophy and theology. Vincent was not satisfied with learning: he meditated on the content of his knowledge at the foot of the crucifix. That was where he prepared his sermons.

Vincent lived during a troubled period in the history of the Church. He was the confessor of Benedict XIII, a pope of Avignon, and he did everything he could so that this pope would put an end to the schism which was tearing the Church apart, but in vain. Recall that there was a Pope in Rome at the same moment. In the last part of his life, from 1400 to 1419, he traveled a large part of Europe as a tireless missionary. Vincent was especially convincing and touched many souls. He was credited with the conversion of 18,000 Muslims, 25,000 Jews, and 40,000 heretics or schismatics, and the return of thousands of Catholics to the practice of their faith.

His style of preaching was simple. He sought to touch the faithful through examples drawn from nature. One day, he mentioned the fact that the birds do four things: they sing, they fly, they wash themselves, and they eat. He drew from this the lesson that we in turn must sing, that is to say praise God; fly, that is to say raise ourselves spiritually; wash ourselves, that is to say purify ourselves through contrition and the sacrament of penance; and finally, while the birds eat earthly food, we must nourish our souls with the Holy

Eucharist. His favorite subject was the four last things. He was the apostle of the Last Judgment.

Vincent was credited with countless miracles. He healed the sick by the hundreds. He passed the last fourteen months of his life in Brittany, sowing everywhere the good word, fortifying the faith of the towns and countryside to last for centuries. As predicted by St. Colette, the great Poor Clare of Besançon, he ended his course at the end of the world, where the universe ends. ["Finistère," the westernmost department of France, is located in the far west of Brittany].

Attributes and patronage

St. Vincent Ferrer is clothed in the white habit and black mantle of the Dominicans. He gives a blessing and holds a book in his hands. Sometimes he also carries in his hands a sun with the letters IHS. He is the patron saint of tilemakers, roofers, plumbers, and glaziers.

Prayer

O God, who hast called a multitude of peoples to the ardor of Thy love and to the fear of Thy judgment, by the salutary preaching of blessed Vincent, Thy Confessor, we beseech Thee, by his merits and intercession, to allow us to appear with confidence in Thy formidable judgment, and to enjoy Thy promises in eternal happiness. Through Our Lord.

—Prayer, *PS*, I, p. 340

Thoughts

- Fear the Lord, and give Him honor, because the hour of His judgment is come.

   —Apocalypse 14:7

- Watch ye, therefore, praying at all times, that you may be accounted worthy to escape all these things that are to come, and to stand before the Son of man.

   —St. Luke 21:36

Resolutions

1 Meditate for ten minutes on the Last Judgment, then recite from the bottom of your heart an act of contrition (See Appendix).

2 See what would trouble us most if we were to appear before God today. Make an appropriate resolution.

3 In temptations, we take refuge in the wounds of Jesus crucified.

St. William of Eskill

April 6

GOD SPEAKS TO US

Blessed is the man that endureth temptation; for when he hath been proved, he shall receive a crown of life.
—Alleluia: St. James 1:12

MEDITATION

William of Eskill (*ca.* 1125-1203) was born near Crépy-en-Valois (Oise). He was educated by his uncle [Hugh], the future abbot of Saint-Germain-des-Prés. William's title of Canon of Saint Genevieve aroused jealousy. He was summoned to leave his confrères but he was soon welcomed by the Augustinian Canons [Regular at the Monastery of Saint Victor, Paris]. Diligent in reading, prayer, and contemplation, he edified his confreres by his uprightness and by his fidelity in observing the rule. Our Lord let him know by revelation that he would soon have to go to an island far from his country where he would have much to suffer, then reassured him by announcing that he would receive a just reward for it in Heaven.

In fact, the Bishop of Roskilde, in Denmark, in need of canons to reform a lax monastery on the island of Eskill, sent William there with three other religious. The monks at that monastery did not view their arrival in a very positive light. However, by his determination, William managed to establish his reform and the monastery was transferred to another island.

After being appointed abbot, William had to face new difficulties. On four occasions his monastery was burnt down. In some years, the harvests were insufficient to meet the needs of his community. The holy religious did not give up, however. He overcame all difficulties with the support of grace and the help of his archbishop. Gradually, he became quite renowned in the Church of Denmark.

He was chosen as intermediary for the marriage of the Princess Ingeborg, sister of King Canute, with Philip

Augustus. Philip had asked the father of his future wife for a very high dowry—which raised the eyebrows of the King of Denmark—but William convinced him to give in. The marriage was contracted on August 14, 1193, but as early as the following day, Philip Augustus wanted to dismiss his wife and have the marriage annulled. William then appealed to Pope Celestine III to demonstrate the lack of foundation for invalidity because of kinship. However, his efforts were unsuccessful. Indeed, it would be necessary to wait until 1213 for Innocent III to impose a ban on the kingdom of France in order to force the king to take back Ingeborg as his wife. William fought for justice until the end of his days, and, at his death on April 6, 1203, he left a prosperous abbey to his successor.

Prayer

May the intercession of blessed Abbot William be a recommendation to us, Lord, and may we obtain by his patronage what we cannot expect from our merits. (Collect)

Thoughts

- But let your speech be yea, yea: no, no: and that which is over and above these, is of evil.

    —St. Matthew 5:37

- Beware of duplicities, artifices, and dissimulations: although it is not good always to tell all kinds of truths, still it is never permissible to contravene the truth.

    —St. Francis de Sales, *IVD*, Book III, ch. 30

Resolutions

1 Examine yourself to see if you have offended in any way by lying, and note it for your next confession.

2 By identifying the circumstances that can lead to lie, make a preventive resolution accordingly.

3 Constantly show that you are upright in your profession.

St. Maria Crescentia

April 7

GOD SPEAKS TO US

That through many tribulations we must enter into the kingdom of God.

—Acts of the Apostles 14:21

MEDITATION

Since God is Providence, He takes care of us, He is interested in us, and He does everything to attract us to Himself. But His ways are not our ways, His plans are not our plans. This is why we have to take paths that often seem disconcerting to us, at least at first glance. The important thing in difficult moments is not to lose confidence. One of the most painful trials here below is to suffer injustice. Our whole being then tends to stiffen, and even perhaps to rebel. To keep our composure it is necessary to go beyond the secondary causes, that is, the external circumstances, to see the hand of God who is shaping our soul in the image of His divine Son.

The life of St. Maria Crescentia Höss (1682-1744) is an example of overcoming injustice. Born in Bavaria (Germany), from the age of five years she consecrated her virginity and, nine years later, her guardian angel presented her with a cross and the habit of St. Francis of Assisi. Nevertheless, she had to endure seven years of hardship from her father and the superior of the convent, because both wanted to prevent her entering religious life. Once she was admitted to the convent, Maria Crescentia suffered from the horrible conduct of her unworthy superior, who went so far as to lock her up in a dark dungeon and to give her barely enough to eat. She accepted all with angelic patience. The superior was finally deposed in 1707 and replaced by Mother Johanna Altneger. She guided the young nun on the way of perfection with strength and sweetness. But when new calumnies against her started to circulate, the saint was excluded from the convent for six months. She accepted this new trial with the spirit of faith. Later, she held the office of portress with great self-denial; then she was chosen as novice mistress in 1726. She held that position before becoming superior of her convent, at the death of Mother Johanna Altneger. From the beginning of her term of office she suffered from poor health, but she still had three years left to spend in this land of exile before departing for Heaven, at Easter 1744.

Saint Maria Crescentia, you who heroically accepted unjust and cruel trials throughout your life, intercede for us with God so that we in turn may carry our cross with serenity and confidence.

Prayer

Hear us, O God our Savior; grant that, in our joy in celebrating the blessed virgin Maria Crescentia, we may also be animated by feelings of fervent piety. Through Jesus Christ. (Collect)

Thoughts

- I want to sacrifice everything and suffer without complaining, since my Jesus prevents me from fearing anything.

    —St. Bernadette, *PPJ*, March 30

- This other thought also did me a lot of good: "Always do what costs us the most." This helped me to overcome several small reluctances.

    —St. Bernadette, *PPJ*, April 22

Resolutions

1 Pray the Fourth Sorrowful Mystery for a person in your circle of acquaintances who is sorely tried.

2 Welcome the annoyances of the day without complaining.

3 Tackle a tedious task that you had been putting off.

St. Walter of Pontoise

April 8

GOD SPEAKS TO US

Jesus saith [to his disciples]: My meat is to do the will of him that sent me, that I may perfect his work.

—St. John 4:34

MEDITATION

Walter (†1092 or 1099) was born in Audainville, Picardy. Considering the penchant that he had for vanity, to nip temptation in the bud he entered the Abbey of Rebais in the Diocese of Meaux. He edified the community by his piety and austerity. His fame went far beyond the framework of his convent, so much so that in Pontoise, monks from a new community chose him as abbot. There he introduced the Rule of St. Benedict. In his governance of souls, he displayed prudence, wisdom, and unction. However, fearing a fall into pride because of his high office, he secretly left his abbey to go to that of Cluny, which was directed by St. Hugh. Walter hid his identity there, but ended up being recognized and was brought back to his Abbey in Pontoise, thanks to the intervention of the Archbishop of Rouen.

His fame continuing to grow, Walter again felt obliged to flee his monastery and reached a small island near Tours. There, he received many visitors, and, one fine day, was recognized by a pilgrim, who conveyed the news to the monks of his community. A delegation from his abbey then begged him to take charge of their foundation again because it was beginning to decline. He yielded to their request, resuming his office with self-denial and generosity. Nevertheless, still aspiring to a more hidden life, he took advantage of a stay in Rome to beg Pope Gregory VII to relieve him of his heavy burden. The Holy Father's response was not the one he expected. The Pope showed him that beyond his personal sanctification, he had a mission to accomplish within the Church. In fact, many disorders were to be repressed thanks to him. Strengthened by the support of the Pope,

Walter reproached King Philip I for carrying on a sacrilegious business with holy things (simony).

He also threw all his weight into enforcing the decision of the Holy See prohibiting the faithful from hearing the Mass of a priest who had a concubine. Finally, he did not hesitate to put the faithful in their place. One day when a distinguished woman entered a church wearing unsuitable clothing, the man of God reprimanded her sharply. This woman, stung in her self-esteem, protested and dared to answer him that the following Sunday, she would put on an even skimpier outfit. The Father Abbot firmly and gravely announced to her that that would not happen. In fact, the Countess of Beaumont fell ill abruptly and died a short time later, on the same day that he did, as he had predicted.

Prayer

May the intercession of Blessed Abbot Walter be a recommendation to us, Lord, and enable us to obtain by his patronage what we cannot expect from our merits. (Collect)

Thoughts

- To know the will of God so as to do it, whatever it is, and to throw ourselves into it with all our heart and with all our strength.

  —Charles de Foucauld, *PPJ*, June 4

- We Christians have received a great light; let us not hide it by shutting it up within ourselves, but let us strive to make it benefit others.

  —Charles de Foucauld, *PPJ*, May 26

Resolutions

1 Accept the place that is yours in the Church and in society without dreaming of another.

2 Know how to use your authority to defend the rights of God, especially in the area of faith and morals.

3 Always wear clothing that is beyond reproach.

St. Mary of Egypt

April 9

God speaks to us

Jesus saith [to the Pharisees]: I am not come to call the just, but sinners.

—St. Matthew 9:13

Meditation

When God communicates sanctifying grace to a soul, He gives her the means of saving her whole life. God's gifts are without repentance. On the day of his baptism a baby receives a white garment, symbol of this grace, and the priest, in giving it to him, invites him to keep it spotless until he comes before the tribunal of God. However, when a soul loses the state of grace by committing a mortal sin, God, in His generosity, offers her a new lifeline. Did Our Lord not exhort us to forgive seventy times seven times? Although it is true that it is preferable never to have committed a single mortal sin, it is important to know that God is mercy and that He welcomes the repentant sinner gladly and wholeheartedly. Unfortunately, someone who commits the sin is the slave of sin. And so, the soul imprisoned by carnal passions, as soon as she is touched by grace, asks how to get out of this vicious circle. St. Mary of Egypt (†421) proved by her life that this is possible.

At the age of twelve, she gave free rein to her unbridled passions, drinking blithely from the cup of sin for seventeen years until the moment when, finding herself in Jerusalem on the day of the Feast of the Exaltation of the Holy Cross, she tried to go into the Church of Calvary to adore the Cross. But three times, she felt that she was driven back.

Touched by grace before an icon of the Blessed Virgin, she wept abundantly for her sins and made the vow to devote herself to penitence if she could reverence the wood of the Holy Cross that was exposed publicly. Immediately, she managed to enter the church and kept her commitment. She then withdrew to the desert for forty-seven years to weep over her sins and implore the grace of God. St. Zosimas, a priest whom she had met providentially, related her story. He brought her Holy Communion one Holy Thursday, and the following year, going back to visit her, he found her dead next to this message written on the sand: "Abbot Zosimas, bury here the body of the sinner Mary. I died the night of Good Friday, shortly after receiving the Holy Mysteries." Zosimas then paid his last respects to her mortal remains.

O Mary of Egypt, pray to God to arouse in my soul sentiments of sincere contrition and holy desires for a better life.

Prayer

Grant us, most clement Father, that blessed Mary of Egypt, who obtained pardon for her sins by loving our Lord Jesus Christ above all, may obtain for us eternal beatitude from Thy mercy. Through the same Jesus Christ. (Collect)

Thoughts

- Embrace the Cross that your Spouse carried, and know that all your efforts must be directed to this noble end.
  —St. Teresa of Avila, *PPJ*, March 30

- What does God do when He looks at a person and takes care of him, if not inflame him with His love, and turn him entirely into His love?
  —Pauline Jaricot, *PPJ*, June 15

Resolutions

1 Pray the First Sorrowful Mystery to beg for the conversion of a sinner.

2 Pray the psalm *Miserere* as a sign of regret for your sins. (See Appendix.)

3 Joyfully remain always in a state of grace.

St. Fulbert of Chartres

April 10

GOD SPEAKS TO US

Jesus saith [to his disciples]: You are the light of the world.
—St. Matthew 5:14

MEDITATION

Fulbert (†1029) studied in Reims under the direction of the future Pope Sylvester II. Much later, Fulbert became chancellor of the Cathedral of Chartres. He is considered as the greatest scholar of his epoch, both in religious matters and in the secular sciences. Upon becoming Bishop of Chartres in 1007, he continued his teaching career, and his school became the most renowned academy in France. In theology, he refuted the heresy of Berengarius concerning the manner of the presence of Christ in the Holy Eucharist.

While being very attached to his diocese, he acquired a reputation that went far beyond this territory. From all over France, people had recourse to his lights. His letters marvelously combined firmness and gentleness. He presented himself with much modesty: he wrote, "I am the very little bishop of a very big Church." On another occasion he declared, "I am filled with miseries, incapable of behaving myself and nevertheless charged with leading others in the ways of salvation." His office sometimes compelled him to use force to reprimand certain abuses; nevertheless, he always admonished politely so as to avoid hurting his interlocutors.

Although he responded to the exterior demands of his diocese, this did not mean that he neglected the care of his own faithful. He preached the good news to them. He especially loved to sing the praises of Our Lady, since he held her in great veneration. He never stopped praising her, inspiring in his followers an enthusiastic devotion to her. They say that one day the Blessed Virgin, to reward him, showed her concern for him by curing him of a very serious illness. She caused a mysterious balm to be poured out on his lips which made the sickness disappear. The holy bishop also wrote hymns and prose works, and undertook the construction of the magnificent cathedral of Chartres, after the fire in 1020. Donations came from everywhere to honor God and to enable the faithful to pray in the midst of beauty. Fulbert's devotion to Our Lady led him to place the building under her patronage. In the crypt, devotees honor Our Lady of the Underground; the story goes that in the time of the Druids, Christians prayed there to the *virgo paritura*, the Virgin who was to give birth.

After heading his diocese for fourteen years, Fulbert rendered his beautiful soul to God.

Prayer

O God, who didst deign to enlighten Thy Church by the merits and teachings of blessed Fulbert, Thy Confessor and Bishop; be favorable to us and grant to us that by his example, applying ourselves to reading and study, we might merit to receive eternal life. Through Our Lord Jesus Christ. (Collect)

Thoughts

- Humility is the disposition which facilitates the free access of the soul to spiritual and divine goods.
  —St. Thomas Aquinas, *PPJ*, March 1

- In every peril, you can obtain the salvation of this glorious Virgin.
  —St. Thomas Aquinas, *PPJ*, October 21

Resolutions

1. Pray the Fifth Glorious Mystery in honor of the Blessed Virgin, concluding with an invocation to Our Lady of Chartres.

2. Decorate with flowers an image of Our Lady.

3. Repeat interiorly the invocation: "Lord, have mercy on me, a poor sinner," when you feel a surge of vanity or pride rising within yourself.

St. Leo the Great

April 11

GOD SPEAKS TO US

If thou lovest me, Simon Peter, feed my lambs, feed my sheep.

—*Cf.* St. John 21:15-17

MEDITATION

The pope's mission is to transmit faithfully and integrally the deposit of faith and to defend his flock against ravenous wolves. In certain troubled epochs of the Church's history, the exercise of this double mission takes on a heroic character. Despite the difficulties, St. Leo the Great (398-461) did not shirk his duties. Born probably in Rome of an important Tuscan family, he was elevated at the age of forty years to the supreme pontificate. The fifth century was particularly eventful. The Pope had to deal with the Manicheans, who affirmed the existence of two creative principles; with the Arians, who denied the divinity of Jesus Christ; with the Priscillianists, who denied the distinction between the Persons in the Trinity; with the Donatists, with the Nestorians, and with the Eutychians, other heretics who were poisoning the Church.

By means of writings, legates, and councils, he resisted all these devastating currents and enabled many wandering sheep to return to the fold, thanks to the clarity of his mind and the determination of his will. In 451, at the Council of Chalcedon, which convened more than six hundred bishops, he defended so well the twofold nature—human and divine—of Our Lord against Eutyches (a monk from Constantinople) that the bishops exclaimed: "Peter has spoken by the voice of Leo!" He opposed both the spiritual enemies of his time and the temporal ones, such as the dreaded Attila. In 452, he stood up to the latter and saved Rome; then, in 455, he opposed the sack of the city by Genseric, king of the Vandals.

The pope also showed his pastoral zeal through

preaching. His sermons were short but well suited to impress minds and touch hearts. Nor did he fail to write to all regions of the empire, which earned him the title of Doctor of the Church. He was rightly regarded as one of the most eminent popes of Christian antiquity, with Gregory the Great; his historical role was crucial. At a time when the whole political order was collapsing in the West and when the religious East was dissolving in controversies concerning Christ, he was able to affirm, achieve, and maintain Christian unity under the supremacy of the Bishop of Rome, the successor of St. Peter.

Attributes

St. Leo is depicted as Pope and Doctor of the Church, with the crozier and the Gospel book.

Prayer

Look benevolently on Thy flock, Eternal Shepherd, and keep it in Thy constant protection, by the intercession of blessed Leo, Thy Supreme Pontiff, whom Thou didst appoint Shepherd of the whole Church. Through Our Lord Jesus Christ. (Collect)

Thoughts

- For the Son of God…has taken on Himself the nature of man, thereby to reconcile it to its Author: in order that the inventor of death, the devil, might be conquered through that nature which he had conquered.

  —St. Leo the Great, Sermon 21

- Christian, acknowledge your dignity, and becoming a partner in the Divine nature, refuse to return to the old baseness by degenerate conduct.

  —St. Leo the Great, Sermon 21

Resolutions

1. Pray the Third Glorious Mystery that the Pope will imitate St. Leo the Great by transmitting the deposit of the faith and by protecting the faithful against the impious world.
2. Meditate for ten minutes on the *Apostles' Creed*. (See Appendix.)
3. Edify your neighbor by your virtues, so as to draw souls of good will to the Church.

St. Gemma Galgani

April 12

GOD SPEAKS TO US

I bear the marks of the Lord Jesus in my body.
—St. Paul to the Galatians 6:17

MEDITATION

Gemma Galgani (1878-1903) was born in Lucca in Tuscany (Italy), into a family of eight children; her father was a pharmacist. She had fine predispositions towards virtue; from the age of two years, she stopped crying. She was of a very even temperament in all circumstances. At the age of five, she already loved to read the breviary. Before being called home by God when Gemma was only eight years old, her mother taught her to love the cross and awakened in her the desire for Heaven.

The following year, after a ten-day retreat during which she made the resolution to live always in the presence of God, Gemma made her First Communion. At the age of seventeen, she stopped going to school in order to take care of her brothers and sisters. She showed a great love for the poor. From then on, she occasionally had apparitions of Our Lord. He encouraged her to bear patiently the vicissitudes of the present life.

Her father died in 1897. Despite a bone disease in her feet which made her suffer cruelly, Gemma took steps to enter a religious community. Due to her failing health, she was turned away from all the congregations. Even when she was physically better, the archbishop intervened to forbid the superior of the Sisters of Saint-Camillus to receive her.

Jesus had told her one day: "Learn to suffer, for suffering teaches to love." She received the stigmata starting in 1899. They would appear around 8:00 p.m. on Thursday and remain until Friday at 3:00 p.m. Discoloration of the back and palm of the hands occurred; then a tearing of the flesh under the skin, which split. The perforations seemed to go clear through her hands, but it was difficult to tell because they filled with blood which partly coagulated. Gemma also endured bloody sweats related to the ordeal of the crowning with thorns.

The machinations of the devil, who did everything he could to try to disturb or seduce her, added to these sufferings. He even went so far as to beat her. Soon her ordeal came to an end. She fell sick in 1902, and Jesus appeared to her to announce to her that she was going to endure very great sufferings to expiate sins committed by priests.

After these sorrows, which she endured with angelic patience, at the age of twenty-five she went to meet her sweet Jesus, on Holy Saturday, April 11, 1903.

Prayer

Hear our prayer, O God Our Savior; grant that, in our joy of celebrating the blessed virgin Gemma, we may also be animated with the sentiments of a fervent piety. Through Jesus Christ. (Collect)

Thoughts

- Let us wait, let us suffer in peace, the hour of rest draws near, the slight tribulations of this momentary life produce in us an eternal weight of glory.
    —St. Thérèse of the Child Jesus, *PPJ*, April 13

- Let us always have our thought fixed on that which is to last eternally, without concerning ourselves with things here below, which disappear even more quickly than we ourselves.
    —St. Teresa of Avila, *PPJ*, November 14

Resolutions

1 Recite a prayer for priests. (See Appendix.)

2 Take refuge in the wounds of Jesus at the moment of temptation.

3 Accept sufferings in the spirit of reparation for your sins, and as a school of charity.

St. Hermenegild

April 13

God speaks to us

For I came to set a man at variance against his father, … and the daughter-in-law against her mother-in-law.
—St. Matthew 10:35

Meditation

Hermenegild (d. 586), son of Liuvigild, king of the Visigoths in Spain, raised in Arianism, married Ingund, the very Catholic daughter of Sigebert I, King of the Franks of Austrasia. Hermenegild's father had married in a second marriage Goiswintha, a profoundly anti-Catholic Arian, from which arose endless disputes between her and Ingund.

In order to have peace, Liuvigild sent the young couple to Seville. There Hermenegild made the acquaintance of Saint Leander, Archbishop of this city, and received from him Holy Baptism to the great joy of Ingund, but to the great displeasure of his father. He did everything to ruin his son. Hermenegild made an alliance with the Emperor of Byzantium against his father. Liuvigild drew his son to him with ostensible gentleness; then, once Hermenegild had been brought back to him, he made Hermenegild wear the clothes of a slave and sent him into exile. Saint Gregory the Great (d. 604) told how Liuvigild then did everything he could to make his son return to Arianism. He used alternatively "the carrot and the stick," caresses and threats. He went so far as to strip Hermenegild of all his possessions. Nevertheless, Hermenegild was so happy and peaceful because he had discovered the true religion that he would not abandon it for anything in the world. Furious, Liuvigild imprisoned him, binding Hermenegild with iron fetters on his neck and hands. This did not disturb Hermenegild, who had agreed to suffer everything to honor Jesus Christ.

As Easter approached, Liuvigild sent Hermenegild an Arian bishop to bring him Holy Communion. Hermenegild, understanding the deception, emphatically refused to receive the Host from the hand of a heretic. His father, mad with rage, ordered his guards to kill Hermenegild. They obeyed his orders, penetrating the prison, and struck the young prisoner on the head with an ax, thus earning Hermenegild the palm of martyrdom.

After his death, people heard chanting near the body of the saint and others saw bright lights there. But above all, his brother Reccared—touched by grace—converted, along with the whole nation of the Goths.

Attributes

Saint Hermenegild is depicted as a tall, handsome young man with a crowned head. He holds in one hand the martyr's palm and in the other the symbol of Christ, Alpha and Omega. He is the patron of Seville.

Prayer

O God, who taught the blessed martyr Hermenegild to put the kingdom of heaven before that of the earth, grant us to despise—as he did—empty possessions and to attach ourselves to eternal possessions. Through Jesus Christ. (Collect)

Thoughts

- It is essential to confess the faith, to bear public witness to it with as much humility and gentleness as with pride and patience.

    —Père Calmel, *365J*, September 17

- The reason why the martyrs are indomitable is because they realize that the treasure which is in them does not come from them, and that consequently they cannot dispose of it.

    —Père Calmel, *365J*, September 2

RESOLUTIONS

1 Recite an Act of Faith (See Appendix).
2 Recite a *Magnificat* to thank God that you know Jesus Christ and His Church (See Appendix).
3 Following the example of Saint Hermenegild, overcome the desire for human respect when faith is at stake in order to witness to the true religion.

St. Justin

April 14

God speaks to us

The wicked have told me fables: but not as thy law, [Lord].
—Introit: Psalm 118:85

Meditation

Justin (d. 166) was born at Nablus in Palestine, probably to a family of Latin colonists. Although reared in a pagan environment, he craved truth and he had an ardent desire to find God. He began by consulting a Stoic, but this man pretended that the knowledge of God was useless. He then turned to another philosopher too interested in fees to hold his attention. He continued his investigation with a Pythagorean who invited him to study music, astronomy, and geometry first, but Justin had no taste for these studies. The disciple of Plato whom Justin consulted a little after held his attention more, although he did not succeed in satisfying him fully. Finally, around the year 130, Justin met an old man who was wisdom incarnate. He made Justin discover the errors and limits of Platonism and know God, the unchanging being, principle, and end of all things. After this first philosophical approach, he revealed to Justin the existence of the prophets, and from there it was just one step to Jesus Christ, whose coming they had announced, and he described His whole life down to the smallest detail. He hastened to show Justin the need to combine study with the practice of humility and prayer so that he might receive the ineffable treasure of the Catholic faith. Excited by these explanations, Justin began to study the Holy Scriptures.

Grace was already at work in his soul, and the attitude of Christians in the face of death finally convinced him. When he began to mix with them, Justin admired them. He realized that their faith enabled them to lead a holy life in the midst of a corrupt world. Their attitude convinced him to embrace Christianity. He in turn wanted to live in a holy way even if he risked his life. From then on, he threw himself into the apostolate with the desire to win souls to Jesus Christ. He defended the Christian cause against Jews and pagans, working as a theologian depending on Sacred Scripture and Tradition to outline various articles of faith. Justin was the first renowned Christian apologist.

In 166, Justin was denounced as a Christian by a rival professor and suffered martyrdom after saying to the prefect Rusticus: "I am a Christian. Our dearest desire is to suffer for Jesus Christ, in order to be saved. This will be our salvation and our security before the more formidable tribunal of our Master and Savior, where the whole world will pass."

Prayer

O God, Who through the foolishness of the cross didst teach the blessed Martyr Justin the surpassing knowledge of Jesus Christ: enable us by his intercession to put away all deceits of error and obtain steadfastness of faith. Through Jesus Christ. (Collect)

Thoughts

- They call us atheists. Yes, certainly, we are atheists of these so-called gods, but we believe in the very true God, Father of justice, wisdom, and other virtues, in whom nothing evil is mixed.
  —St. Justin, First Apologia, 6

- We adore and we love the Word born of the eternal and ineffable God, since He was made man for us, in order to heal us of all our ills by taking part in them.
  —St. Justin, Second Apologia, 13

Resolutions

1 Pray the First Glorious Mystery, asking for faith.

2 Rather than scattering your attention by surfing the internet, study Catholic doctrine in depth so as to spread it better.

3 Practice constantly the Christian virtues in order to arouse the desire for faith in souls of good will.

St. Peter González

April 15

God speaks to us

Hath not God made foolish the wisdom of this world?
—First Epistle of Saint Paul to the Corinthians 1:20

Meditation

To awaken a vocation, sometimes the good Lord inclines the will of young people to give themselves to Him, sometimes He uses His ministers, or else He resorts to external events. For some souls the trials of life are the occasion to come to their senses and to realize the nothingness of earthly realities compared to spiritual goods.

The Spaniard Peter González (*ca*. 1190-1246) experienced this. He grew up in a wealthy milieu and developed his human qualities; nevertheless, he let himself be won over by a worldly, thoughtless, superficial spirit. His maternal uncle, the Bishop of Astorga, named him as a canon and soon after a dean of the cathedral chapter. On Christmas Day Peter, driven by vanity, climbed on a richly adorned horse and crossed the city of Astorga to the applause of the crowd. But soon the animal, stumbling, threw the rider into the mud to the mocking laughter of the crowd. Upset and seething with anger, he exclaimed: "O traitor world, you mocked me; I will mock you." On the spot, he decided to become a religious. He was soon admitted to the Dominican Order and led an edifying life among them. He studied the Sacred Scriptures thoroughly, and acquired in a short time the virtues of humility, chastity, and penance. One day when men tried to corrupt him by bringing him a woman of ill repute, far from letting himself be seduced, he converted her.

His sermons were remarkable. He was as much at ease in the court of King (Saint) Ferdinand III—who chose him as an adviser—as he was with the poor and the peasants of Galicia and Asturias. He received the nickname of "new apostle of Spain." Enriched by the gift of miracles, Peter saved from a storm some sailors who had invoked him, and he warded off a violent storm with his prayers, to the satisfaction of the faithful who had come to the countryside to listen to his preaching. He was also credited with building a bridge in Portugal.

Worn out by his apostolic labors, Peter died in 1246, on Palm Sunday.

Attributes, invocation, and patronage

Saint Peter González, who is known in Spain under the name of Saint Elmo, is depicted walking on the water and holding a flame in his hands. He is invoked against earthquakes. He is the patron of navigators and sailors.

Prayer

O God, Who dost gladden us by the annual solemnity of blessed Peter, Thy confessor, deign to ensure that while celebrating his birth in Heaven we also imitate the example of his life. Through Jesus Christ. (Collect)

Thoughts

- Use caution with the evil world, and you will live always in the solitude of your soul.

  —St. Francis Xavier, *PPJ*, June 20

- Do not think that our advancement depends on some other unknown and extraordinary method; no, all our good consists in the perfect conformity of our will with the will of God.

  —St. Teresa of Avila, *PPJ*, May 8

Resolutions

1 Pray the First Joyful Mystery to ask God to stir up a vocation in your home.

2 From the least movement of vanity, pray an ejaculatory prayer, for example: "Lord, have mercy on me."

3 Let others speak in society; take an interest in those who are lonely.

St. Benedict-Joseph Labre

April 16

God speaks to us

Who is as the Lord our God, who dwelleth on high: And looketh down on the low things in heaven and in earth?

—Psalm 112:5-6

Meditation

God, in His goodness towards His creatures, looks kindly upon the weakest, the humblest on the earth, in order to raise them, to draw them to Himself, and to surround them with honor and glory. He wanted in this way to bring men to extinguish the fire of the lust of the eyes, the lust of the flesh, and the pride of life which is at the root of all their evils. He gave this great lesson through his servant Benedict-Joseph Labre (1748-1783).

The eldest of fifteen children, he was born in Amettes (Pas-de-Calais) into a family of deeply Catholic peasants. As a small boy, Benedict-Joseph loved to serve Mass and showed a great devotion to the Holy Eucharist. Two priest uncles were in charge of completing his education. However, although he had a gift for learning theology, he had no talent for academic work. Thinking to become a religious, he knocked on the door of various Carthusian or Trappist monasteries. The response was invariably the same: "Providence has not called you to the religious life, follow divine inspiration." At the age of twenty-two, moved by an interior light, Benedict-Joseph departed on a pilgrimage. During the remaining thirteen years of his life, he traveled more than 30,000 kilometers (18,600 miles), visiting different sanctuaries of France, Italy, Switzerland, and Spain. By his way of life he was the apostle of humility, poverty, mortification, and penitence. By his silence he condemned useless chatter, malicious gossip, and calumnies; his rags stigmatized unbridled luxury and his fasting, excesses of eating and drinking. By sleeping under a staircase or on the bare earth, he reproached the softness of the age. Refusing money, Benedict begged for bread and spent most of the day before the Blessed Sacrament. He was always smiling, he who, before finding his way, had been prone to anxiety and scruples. In order to authenticate his virtue, God gave him the gift of miracles, visions, revelations, and bilocation. At the age of thirty-five, he died in Rome on a straw mat, in a butcher's loft, and the crowds immediately flocked to his mortal remains, proclaiming his holiness.

Patronage

Saint Benedict Joseph Labre is the patron of beggars and pilgrims.

Prayer

O God, Who didst make Thy holy Confessor Benedict Joseph, by the pursuit of humility and by the love of poverty, cleave unto Thee alone: grant us by the help of his merits to despise all earthly things and ever to seek those of heaven. Through Jesus Christ. (Collect)

Thoughts

- The pilgrim who goes merrily and sings on his journey overcomes boredom and lightens the difficulty of the journey.

    —St. Francis de Sales, *PPJ*, August 8

- Love the poor and poverty, for by this love you will become truly poor, since we are made like the things we love.

    —St. Francis de Sales, *PPJ*, September 27

RESOLUTIONS

1. Plan to stop at a place of pilgrimage on your next trip. Until then visit your parish church.
2. Accept poverty without envying riches, if that is your social situation.
3. Help the poor according to your means. See Jesus in them, and be kind to them, if you can't help them more.

St. Louis-Marie de Montfort

April 17 (celebrated on the 28th)

GOD SPEAKS TO US

He was directed by God unto the repentance of the nation, and he took away the abominations of wickedness. And he directed his heart towards the Lord, and in the days of sinners he strengthened godliness.

—Ecclesiasticus 49:3-4

MEDITATION

Born in Brittany, in Montfort-sur-Meu, Louis-Marie Grignion (1673-1716) shared the tenacity characteristic of his region. Being straightforward, he was not considerate to a fault: he went straight to the point, and was incapable of yielding. When grace perfected nature, he joined to his natural strength a great sweetness permitting him—once ordained a priest—to win hearts. His artistic soul manifested itself in popular songs that he composed; his intelligence was penetrating, luminous, original; his language colorful. To subdue the old man, to fight the attacks of the devil, and to make reparation for the sins of men, he had recourse to penance. Privations, fasts, sleepless nights, hair shirts, joined to ardent prayer, guaranteed the success of his apostolate. "God alone!" was his motto. Louis-Marie suffered from seeing Jesus so unloved, He who was so good! Louis-Marie's humility was so great, his love for the poor and for the cross so profound, that his superiors accused him of singularity and extravagance. It was because he was affected by the folly of the cross, which is wisdom in the eyes of God. In his apostolate he was like Our Lord, a sign of contradiction, for he preached the Gospel without respect of persons, without convolutions or carefully chosen words. God helped him to perform miracles so as to confirm his teaching. His preferred topics were the Sacred Heart, the cross of Jesus, and the Blessed Virgin. Admired by some, he was detested by others. Nevertheless, the more he met with opposition, the more his ministry flourished. At Pontchâteau, he erected a magnificent Calvary, but the day before its blessing, he received from the episcopal authority the express prohibition to proceed with it, and the court forced him to destroy it. Happily, one day his work would be restored.

In Brittany, in the Vendée, in Anjou, in Normandy, in Saintonge, he organized missions that revived the faith and saved charity. He was the founder of the Montfort Fathers and the Daughters of Wisdom. Since Marian devotion was his dominant passion, in the midst of his extremely active life he wrote the *Treatise on True Devotion to the Blessed Virgin*. Worn out by his work and his mortifications, he died at the age of forty-three, in Saint-Laurent-sur-Sèvre, in the Vendée.

Prayer

O God, Who didst make Saint Louis-Marie an eminent herald of the kingdom of Thy beloved Son and through him gavest to Thy Church two new religious congregations: Through his counsels and merits and under the sweet yoke of the most Blessed Virgin, his Mother, may we ever serve Thy beloved Son. Who with Thee liveth and reigneth. (Collect)

Thoughts

- To know Jesus Christ, the incarnate Wisdom, is to know enough; to know everything and not to know Him, is to know nothing.

  —St. Louis-Marie, *ASE*, no 11

- We must give ourselves over to the spirit of Mary in order to be moved and however she likes.… In each action we must take note of how Mary did it or would do it, if she were in our place.

  —St. Louis-Marie, *VD*, no 259

RESOLUTIONS

1. Pray the Litany of the Blessed Virgin in her honor. (See Appendix)
2. Before beginning your work, draw inspiration from the conduct of the Blessed Virgin, so as to imitate her.
3. Read the *Treatise on True Devotion to the Blessed Virgin*.

St. Marie of the Incarnation

April 18

GOD SPEAKS TO US

The woman that feareth the Lord, she shall be praised. Give her of the fruit of her hands: and let her works praise her in the gates.

—Proverbs 31:30-31

MEDITATION

Barbara Avrillot (1565-1618) was born in Paris. Her father was a judge at the Revenue Court. Until Barbara was seven years old, her mother dressed her in white in memory of the beautiful day of her baptism. At the age of eleven, she entered as a boarder at the Abbey of Longchamp founded by Saint Isabelle of France, sister of Saint Louis. She made her First Communion there the following year with great fervor. When she was eighteen years old, despite her attraction to the religious life, at the request of her parents, she married Pierre Acarie de Villemor, a tax collector, a very pious and generous man. Three boys and three girls were born of their union. Madame Acarie raised them in the sight of God, instilling in them a taste for prayer and work. "I will love you as much as you love God," she told them. She had no other ambition for them than to make them virtuous, for she knew that if they were faithful to grace, God would not fail to call them to the state of life to which they were suited. Her three daughters became Carmelites, one of the boys would be a priest, and the two others, a magistrate and a military man. Her husband supported the [Catholic] League, which got them into trouble. Their possessions were confiscated.

Madame Acarie saw to it that her servants did not neglect the interests of the soul; they accompanied her to Mass. She had the gift of receiving confidences from numerous people, for she knew how to take the time to listen to them patiently. Feeling loved, her interlocutors opened up easily, and God enabled her to calm them with her advice. The heretics filled her with pity and she strove to convert them. Madame Acarie suffered heroically. One day, in falling off her horse, she broke a leg and underwent a painful treatment without uttering a single cry, to the great astonishment of the surgeon.

When Saint Teresa of Avila came to reform Carmel in Spain, Madame Acarie urged Cardinal Bérulle to establish it in France, meriting the name of *Foundress of the Carmelites in France*. After the death of her husband, she entered the Order herself as a simple converse sister, and pronounced her vows in 1615 under the name of Sister Marie of the Incarnation. She humbly placed herself under orders of her eldest daughter, the sub-prioress, then she was taken to heaven three years later, on Easter Day, at the Carmel of Pontoise.

Prayer

O God, who didst inspire Blessed Marie with an ardent zeal for Thy glory and with admirable courage in misfortune, grant us, by her intercession, the grace to bear courageously all the adversities, and to persevere in the love of Thy holy religion. Through Our Lord Jesus Christ. (Collect)

Thoughts

- The bucket of a well does not fill unless it is lowered; for myself, I remain empty for lack of lowering myself.
  —Blessed Marie of the Incarnation
- What I suffer is nothing in comparison with what I would like to suffer, and yet what sufferings! My God, have mercy on me.
  —Blessed Marie of the Incarnation

Resolutions

1 Pray the Litany of Humility. (See Appendix)

2 Help the children not to forget their morning prayer so that they will be under God's protection every day.

3 Give some of your time to someone who needs to pour out his feelings to an attentive ear.

St. Peter-Mary Chanel

April 19 (celebrated on the 28th)

God speaks to us

And I will set a sign among them, and I will send of them that shall be saved, to the Gentiles into the sea ... to them that have not heard of me, and have not seen my glory. And they shall declare my glory to the Gentiles, [says the Lord].

—Introit: Isaias 66:19

Meditation

Consecrated to the Blessed Virgin before his birth, Peter-Mary Chanel (1803-1841) was born in the diocese of Belley. After shepherding his parents' flock, he studied Latin under the guidance of Father Trompier. At the minor seminary as at the major seminary, he was an example for his fellow students. Ordained a priest in 1827, Peter-Mary was appointed vicar at Ambérieux, then pastor at Crozet, near Geneva. Very mortified, he observed a strict rule as to times of prayer and of study, but he aspired to another type of life. Thus, after having taught at the minor seminary in Belley, Peter-Mary left in 1836 for Oceania as a member of the newly founded Society of Mary. He embarked at Le Havre on Christmas Eve. During the voyage his virtues, notably his great simplicity, were plain for all the voyagers to see. Arriving at the island of Futuna, he was well received by the king. He learned the language and one month later celebrated Mass for the first time, on the feast of the Immaculate Conception. His success was meager during his three years of apostolate. Peter-Mary endured everything patiently: the scorn, the hazards, the hunger. One day, when the opposition to his ministry became fiercer, the brother who accompanied him said: "Why work? We're going to die tomorrow." The saint replied to him: "If what you say is true, it will not be the worst of our days." With greater calm, he continued to hoe his garden.

As the Gospel made progress, bloody persecution approached. The son of the king himself converted. The king and most of his chiefs were disturbed about this. Having convinced the king to kill the saintly missionary, the minister Musumusu entered the hut of Father Chanel, mistreated him, then one of the chiefs who had supported Father Chanel prepared to deal him a blow on the head with a club. The missionary protected his head with his arm, which broke under the blow, while another intruder pushed the tip of his spear into Father Chanel's chest. Finally, Musumusu himself finished him off by driving an ax into his skull.

The heroic death of the saint led very quickly to the conversion of the island and the suppression of cannibalism, paganism, and idolatry. Musumusu ended by regretting his crime and by himself converting. Numerous healings took place at the holy martyr's tomb.

Prayer

O God, Who hast adorned blessed Peter-Mary, Thy martyr, with admirable sweetness, glowing charity, and an invincible constancy to preach Thy Gospel: grant us, we pray Thee, that in following these examples, we will hold the faith that we profess until death. Through Jesus Christ. (Collect)

Thoughts

- The greater our spirit of sacrifice, the more we will have success in the most desperate situations.
  —St. Peter-Mary Chanel

- Knock on the door of the heart of Mary and you will bring out swarms of missionaries.
 —St. Peter-Mary Chanel, *Letter to a confrere in France*

Resolutions

1 Pray the Third Glorious Mystery for the members of the "Church of silence" in Muslim countries.

2 Strive to be an example to those close to you and your colleagues, and show gentleness by patiently bearing with people who can be irritating.

3 Offer a sacrifice to obtain the conversion of an unbeliever.

St. Agnes de Montepulciano

April 20

GOD SPEAKS TO US

How good is God to them that are of a right heart!
—Psalm 72:1

MEDITATION

Agnes was born in 1274, in Italy, into a rich family adorned with Christian virtues. When she was very little, she enjoyed reciting the *Ave Maria* and retreating to a corner of the garden to pray to Jesus, whom she loved tenderly. Her heart was so pure that she lived very close to God. One day, she went with some friends on a pilgrimage to Montepulciano. Not far from there was a house of ill repute haunted by evil spirits; they attacked her, being unable to countenance her purity. When she was ten or twelve years old, she asked her parents for permission to enter a monastery of virgins. Faced with their refusal because her age, she begged Jesus to remove the obstacles, and was welcomed by the Sacco nuns, who followed the Rule of Saint Augustine. A prayerful soul, she was inclined towards spiritual realities. However, to test her, her superiors assigned her the role of steward. Far from complaining, she performed her tasks perfectly. Her reputation for sanctity began to spread, and some Catholics wanted her build a monastery nearby in Montepulciano. Agnes was only fifteen years old at the time.

All was admirable in her life: her soul sought only to please God, and God in return devised to make her happy through the most touching graces. One night, the Blessed Virgin placed the Child Jesus in her arms, flooding her soul with happiness. At the moment when Our Lady was about to leave her, Agnes unfastened a cross from the string of pearls that Jesus wore around his neck. Although she had her head in Heaven, she had her feet on the ground.

For the building of the monastery, she supervised the construction, and lent a hand in the work. While working, she wore secular clothing, and immediately after, she dressed in the white habit of Saint Dominic. Twenty young girls joined her then to live under her direction. Since God tests those whom He loves, the community found itself without bread for three days, but soon He inspired a Catholic soul to bring her five loaves. While the saint distributed them, they multiplied to the point that they satisfied the entire community for several meals.

Agnes as well acquainted with sorrows, infirmities, and anxieties during the painful illness that eventually carried her off. However, far from worrying about her approaching death, she immersed in profound joy. At midnight, April 20, 1317, she met her Divine Spouse.

Prayer

O God, who hast deigned frequently to water the blessed Agnes Thy virgin with a celestial dew, and to adorn the places where she prayed with various blooming flowers, grant in Thy goodness that, through her prayers, we may continually be fruitful through the rain of Thy blessings, and deserve to reap its fruits for eternity. Through Our Lord. (Collect)

Thoughts

- To be a spouse, is to have your eyes fixed on His, your heart completely captured, completely invaded, as though beside yourself and passing into Him, your soul full of His soul, full of His prayer, your whole being captivated and given.

  —Elisabeth of the Trinity, *PPJ*, May 23

- Pray, pray, or else misfortunes and calamities will fall upon us.

  —St. Agnes

Resolutions

1 Meditate for ten minutes on the life of Saint Agnes, and seek, like her, to have your head in Heaven and your feet on the ground.

2 Keep purity of heart in order to facilitate your union with God.

3 In trials, turn with confidence to Divine Providence.

St. Anselm
April 21

God speaks to us

Nations shall declare his wisdom, and the church shall shew forth his praise.

—Ecclesiasticus 39:14

Meditation

Anselm (1034-1109) was born in Aosta (Italy), to a mother who was very pious and an exemplary educator. To give him a glimpse at the majesty and goodness of God, she showed him the summit of the mountains, surrounded by blue sky, and she told him that that is the beginning of the kingdom of God. She entrusted him at first to a stern teacher, so that Anselm quickly lost his *joie de vivre* and his good nature, to the great anxiety of his mother who then put him into the hands of the Benedictines. The religious developed his scientific mind and his piety. At fifteen years of age, he wanted to become a religious, but his father violently opposed this, for Anselm was his only son. Forced to stay in the world, he let himself be seduced by it, leading a frivolous life for a while. The premature death of his mother increased his distraction, despite the efforts of his father to bring him back to the right path. Faced with family tensions, Anselm decided to move away. He left Italy for France.

Putting an end to his growing disorders, Anselm knocked at the door of the Benedictine Abbey in Bec, in Normandy, and there he completed his studies and entered the monastic life. Named prior, then abbot, he was subsequently chosen Archbishop of Canterbury, in England. At that time he got into trouble with King William the Conqueror, then with his son William II. He asked them for the restitution of the property of the Church of Canterbury, which had been unjustly confiscated. He was forced to go into exile for his relentless defense of the liberty of the Church, once under the reign of William II, and another time under that of Henry I, his successor. In 1106, Henry I ended up renouncing ecclesiastical investiture, which was an abuse of power, since it had to be given by the Pope. Anselm lived subsequently several years in peace in his diocese until the age of seventy-five, where the good Lord called him.

No life was more filled with pitfalls than Anselm's, and yet, despite the ordeal, the contradictions, and the continual illnesses, he found the time to write theological treatises on predestination, grace and free will, the Incarnation, as well as very beautiful meditations and graceful hymns in honor of Our Lady.

O Saint Anselm, pray to God to uphold me so that I in turn may lead a life fruitful in good deeds.

Attributes

He is depicted as a bishop and doctor of the Church, contemplating the apparition of the Infant Jesus and the Blessed Virgin.

Prayer

O God, Who didst give blessed Anselm to Thy people as a minister of eternal salvation: grant, we beseech Thee, that we, who have had him for our teacher on earth, may deserve to have him for our advocate in heaven. Through our Lord. (Collect)

Thoughts

- All that I am I owe to my mother and to the Benedictine monks.

—St. Anselm

- Christ does not want a servile spouse; he loves nothing so much in this world as the freedom of His Church.

—St. Anselm

Resolutions

1 Pray the Second Joyful Mystery to ask God to bless our mother for all that we owe her.

2 Be sure to choose your children's educators prudently.

3 Avoid wasting time, especially on the telephone and on the internet, so as to have maximum presence of mind and to be able to make our life as productive as possible.

Sts. Soter and Caïus

April 22

God speaks to us

I have declared thy justice in a great church, lo, I will not restrain my lips: O Lord, thou knowest it.

—Tract: Psalm 39:10

Meditation

Popes separated by a century, Saints Soter and Caïus both witnessed to the truth of the Catholic faith by shedding their blood for love of Jesus Christ, the divine model. The first thirty popes indeed paid with their lives for the honor of having been elevated to the See of Peter.

Saint Soter (d. 175), born in Fondi (Italy), succeeded Pope Anicetus around the year 166. Thanks to a letter that arrived from the Church of Corinth, we know that he was generous with his aid to the Churches of various cities; he supported the Christians with his advice, exhorting them to remain firm in the faith and to remain united with the priests and bishops who governed them. He showed his charity especially to those who, for their attachment to Our Lord, endured persecution in prison and in the mines. It is also thought that, during the eight or nine years of his pontificate, he energetically opposed the Montanists, whose heresy had begun to crop up. He died a victim of the persecution of Marcus Aurelius.

As for Saint Caïus (d. 295), his pontificate lasted twelve years. He decreed that, to be a holy bishop, one would have to go beforehand through the minor orders of porter, lector, exorcist, and acolyte, and the major orders of subdeacon, deacon, and priest.

Saint Gregory gave the reason: "order should be observed in ascending to orders. For he seeks a fall who aspires to mount to the summit by overpassing the steps."[8] Caïus was

---

[8] Saint Gregory, cited by Saint Thomas Aquinas in the *Summa theologica*, II-II, q. 189, a. 1, ad 3.

put to death during the terrible persecution of Diocletian, after having consecrated five bishops, and ordained twenty-five priests and eight deacons.

"O holy pontiffs…By imitating him in laying down your lives for your sheep, you have taught us how we also should think no sacrifice too great to be made for our faith. Obtain for us this heroic courage."[9]

Prayer

Look forgivingly on Thy flock, Eternal Shepherd, and keep it in Thy constant protection, by the intercession of blessed sovereign pontiffs Soter and Caïus, whom Thou didst constitute Shepherd of the whole Church. Through our Lord. (Collect)

Thoughts

- Like a vigilant mother, the Church, in promoting candidates for the priesthood by various degrees separated by long intervals, does not spare her exhortations to holiness.

  —St. Pius X, *HA*

- For us, considering [the] perils of the soul much superior to those of the body, we find it more sure and more certain to confront physical dangers than to be surprised by God in spiritual dangers.

  —St. Francis Xavier, *PPJ*, December 28

Resolutions

1 Pray the First Joyful Mystery that seminarians may become conscious of the sublimity of their vocation and receive the grace of perseverance.

2 Read a page of the catechism to support your faith.

3 Enlighten people who doubt the existence of God or His goodness towards us.

---

[9] Dom Guéranger, *The Liturgical Year, TP,* II, p. English translation, p. 332

St. George
April 23

GOD SPEAKS TO US

For God hath not given us the spirit of fear: but of power.
—Second Epistle of St. Paul to Timothy 1:7

MEDITATION

Every Catholic is born for a full-scale war against powerful and dreadful enemies. Every Catholic is called to conquer a crown, and to merit it, he must survive the obstacles encountered along the way of duty and virtue. In order to achieve this, he needs courage. Saint George (d. 303) showed throughout his life this disposition of soul, the result of strong convictions.

Born in Lydda, Palestine, George's main virtue was strength. A good captain, after a short time he was named a tribune in Diocletian's army. The Emperor raised him to the rank of senator, which opened to him the doors of the imperial council. Fortune smiled on George when he was twenty years old. But now Diocletian, wishing for the death of Christians, consulted the members of his council on this subject. George, with his brief, forceful, yet modest words, refuted the accusations made against the Christians. His discourse impressed the other members of the council, which worried Diocletian. Furious at this unexpected reaction, Diocletian ordered George to be arrested and thrown into a dungeon.

George was then subjected to various tortures. His body was rolled under a large stone to grind and crush him, then he was mangled by a gearwheel; a heavenly voice sustained him. He was then led before the Emperor. Wishing to respond now, not by words, but by acts, he asked to go to the temple to see the gods to whom he was asked to sacrifice. They led him there. Before the statue of Apollo he said: "Do you want me to make sacrifices to you as God?" The demon present in the statue responded to him: "I am not God, and there is no other God than the one you preach."

And the statue crumbled into dust. The Emperor, furious, decided then to behead our hero, who thus merited the title of "great martyr" given by the Greeks.

O Saint George, valiant soldier, support me in the battleground of life.

Attributes, invocation, and patronage

Saint George is depicted conquering a dragon, often in the form of a knight. He is invoked against sores. He is the patron of knights and of regiments of dragoons.

Prayer

All of Christendom needs, O George, to remember the homages that she lavished on you in days gone by. The ancient piety towards you has, alas! cooled, and for many Christians your feast day goes unnoticed…Have pity on this world in which error has been sown, and which is at this moment in such terrible convulsions.

—Dom Guéranger, *AL*, TP, II, p. 434.

Thoughts

- A Christian should always be ready for combat. As in time of war, there are always sentinels placed here and there to watch for the approach of the enemy; also, we ought to be always on our guard, to see whether the enemy is setting traps for us, and is coming to take us by surprise.

—St. John Vianney, the Curé d'Ars, *PPJ1*, September 9

- It is not always in the power of the soul not to feel temptation, although it is always in its power not to consent to it.

—St. Francis de Sales, *PPJ*, October 20

Resolutions

1 Pray a *Salve Regina* for those who, in our country, endure persecution on account of their faith. (See Appendix.)

2 Let us ask Saint George for the strength to resist the "group-think" propagated by the media.

3 Show the virtue of fortitude by generously and constantly carrying out the duties of your state of life.

St. Fidelis of Sigmaringen

April 24

God speaks to us

Be thou faithful until death: and I will give thee the crown of life.

—Apocalypse 2:10

Meditation

Fidelis (1577-1622) was born in Sigmaringen, a German city near Switzerland. He studied in Freiburg-im-Breisgau (Germany), and he earned the title Doctor of Civil and Ecclesiastical Law. After settling in Colmar, he practiced law for several years, a profession in which he excelled. However, seeing the difficulty of reconciling a life of ease in the world with the demands of the Catholic faith, he aspired to a more perfect life. This led him to leave the world at the age of thirty-five to become a Capuchin. During the first years of his religious life, he enjoyed great spiritual consolations, but soon he found himself assailed by scruples about his vocation. His spiritual director finally enlightened him, enabling him to find strength and peace again. He then sold all his possessions and gave them to charity; stripped of everything he could fully enjoy divine intimacy.

Ordained to the priesthood, Fidelis placed his talents as an orator at the service of the Faith. By his preaching, he awoke the fervor of Catholics and brought about the conversion of Protestants. Indeed, since the Congregation of the Propaganda Fide, founded by Pope Gregory XV, hoped that zealous missionaries would struggle against Calvinism in Switzerland, Saint Fidelis was sent to head the mission in the canton of Grisons. As Dom Guéranger would remark, "Protestantism was established and maintained by the shedding of torrents of blood; and yet Protestants count it as a great crime that, here and there, the children of the true

Church made an armed resistance against them...A Catholic who gives heretics credit for sincerity when they talk about religious toleration, proves that he knows nothing of either the past or the present. There is a fatal instinct in error, which leads it to hate the Truth; and the true Church, by its unchangeableness, is a perpetual reproach to them that refuse to be her children."[10]

Saint Fidelis would experience it. Annoyed by his peaceful conquests, and furious that he had confounded them, the Protestants, short on arguments, decided to kill him. The friar had been praying for a long time to obtain the grace of martyrdom. His prayer would be answered. While he was exhorting Catholics to remain attached to their faith, a troop of Calvinist soldiers invaded his parish on April 24, 1622, and ordered him to become Protestant. The saint repeated before them the profession of Catholic faith in saying: "I did not come to embrace heresy, but to combat it." Raving mad, they pounced on Fidelis and pierced him with daggers.

Prayer

O God, Who didst vouchsafe to inflame the heart of blessed Fidelis with seraphic ardor and to adorn him with the palm of martyrdom and with glorious miracles in spreading the true Faith: we beseech Thee, by his merits and intercession, so to strengthen us in faith and in charity by the might of Thy grace, that we may deserve to be found faithful in Thy service even unto death. Through our Lord. (Collect)

Thoughts

- I ask only two things of God: one, to leave this world without sins, the other, to shed my blood for the Church.

    —St. Fidelis *Pa. S.*, IV, p. 549

- What a misfortune if I fought feebly under a leader crowned with thorns!'

    —St. Fidelis

---

[10] Dom Guéranger, *Liturgical Year*, TP, II, pp. 341-42.

Resolutions

1 Pray the Third Sorrowful Mystery to ask God for the grace to overcome the moral trials of today.

2 Give a good book to a less fortunate person to support him spiritually.

3 Offer a sacrifice to beg God for the conversion of a Protestant.

St. Mark

April 25

GOD SPEAKS TO US

And after these things the Lord appointed also seventy-two others: and he sent them two and two before his face into every city and place whither he himself was to come.

—Gospel of Saint Luke 10:1

MEDITATION

We have no precise information about the youth of Saint Mark. What is certain is that he accompanied Peter on his apostolic voyages "as disciple and as interpreter," says Saint Jerome. When the head of the Apostles preached for the first time in Rome, an immense crowd came to listen to him and were touched by the simplicity and sublimity of the truths taught. As the Apostle could not address each one, the faithful turned to Mark and begged him to continue his stories, which became his Gospel. When we study it, it becomes obvious that Mark is Jewish and that he belongs to Peter's immediate circle of followers.

Later, Mark left Italy to go to Africa. He visited Libya, the northern part of Ethiopia, and all of Egypt, performing many miracles. He settled in Alexandria, in Egypt, where the pagans, irritated by his success, dragged him with a rope around his neck over rocky terrain, then they threw him in prison where he was comforted by an angel. The next day, dragged again into the city, Mark gained the palm of martyrdom after saying: "Lord, into Thy hands I commend my soul." His relics were transferred from Alexandria to Venice.

The symbol of Mark's Gospel is a lion, for it begins with the episode of John the Baptist who, like a roaring lion, cries out in the desert. Mark was strongly influenced by the thought, the inspiration, and the presence of Saint Peter. Saint Mark refers to Peter in person in the healing of his mother-in-law (1:29), in the raising of the daughter of Jairus (5:37), and in the prediction of the destruction of Jerusalem (13:3). Above all, Mark neglects Peter's glories and dwells on his faults. He shows Peter incurring this harsh reply: "Get behind me, Satan!" (8:33) and being reprimanded for sleeping in the Garden of Olives (14:37). Finally, Mark forgot none of the circumstances of Peter's denial.

In his Gospel, we still find the practical spirit of Saint Peter: a lot of deeds, less doctrine. He addresses pagans, especially Romans, hence the details he gives on Jewish customs. We come across few new facts in Mark's writing, but it contains its own wealth.

Attribute, invocation, and patronage

The attribute of Saint Mark is a lion. He is invoked against final impenitence and skin disease. He is the patron of notaries and scribes and also of the city of Venice.

Prayer

O God, Who didst exalt blessed Mark, Thine Evangelist, by the grace of preaching the Gospel, grant, we beseech Thee, that we may ever profit by his teaching and be defended by his prayers. Through our Lord. (Collect)

Thoughts

- Jesus said to them: Go ye into the whole world, and preach the gospel to every creature.

—St. Mark 16:15

- And he said: So is the kingdom of God, as if a man should cast seed into the earth, and should sleep, and rise, night and day, and the seed should spring, and grow up whilst he knoweth not.

—St. Mark 4:26-27

Resolutions

1 Pray the First Glorious Mystery to ask of Our Lady the return of our country to the Faith.

2 Read a chapter of the Gospel according to Saint Mark.

3 Acknowledge your faults without seeking to make false excuses.

St. Zita

April 26 (celebrated the 27th)

God speaks to us

So let your light shine before men, that they may see your good works, and glorify your Father who is in heaven.
—St. Matthew 5:16

Meditation

Zita (1210-1278) was born near Lucca, in Tuscany (Italy). From her earliest childhood, she had only one desire: to please God. It sufficed for her teachers to tell her: "This pleases God, this does not please God," to dictate her behavior. When she was twelve years old, her father sent her out to sell fruits on the streets of Lucca. The gentleness of his daughter drew buyers so well that she always returned home with an empty basket. Six years later, she became a servant at the home of the Farinelli, a noble family from her home town. Although more in contact with the world, she completely preserved her virtue, manifesting in particular her overflowing charity towards the poor. Not content to pass on to them the gifts from her mistress, she fasted daily to give them her own food. All that she demanded of Signora Farinelli was to be able to pray every morning in the nearest church.

One day, lost in her prayer, she did not notice the time pass. Disconcerted, she said that she would not have time to make bread for the family, but, O miracle! The bread had been kneaded by the angels. Another time, she offered to a pilgrim a glass of water and blessed it. The man drank with delight, for the water had changed into a delicious wine. Her life was thus woven with miracles in the service of charity.

As life here below cannot pass without trials, Zita was not spared. One day, a servant, smitten with her beauty, allowed himself to be too familiar with her. Zita, so sweet, defended herself by scratching his face with her fingernails, to the great disappointment of the overly aggressive gallant. Her virtue also aroused jealousy on the part of her co-workers, who spoke ill of Zita in front of her mistress. The mistress, a little too credulous, reprimanded her servant, who deferred to her without saying a word. Happily, the mistress finally recognized Zita's innocence and rewarded her by permitting Zita to end her days at her home. The more Zita approached the end of her life, the more she detached herself from the world. She was sick five days then passed away in the greatest calm, happy to join her divine Savior in Heaven.

Attributes, invocation, and patronage

Saint Zita has for attributes a bunch of keys and a pitcher. She is the patroness of housemaids, servants, and the city of Lucca.

Prayer

O God, Who hast transported the blessed virgin Zita from her humble state of servant to the eternal kingdom, grant us, by her intercession, that after having served Thee faithfully on the earth, we may merit to be glorified with her in heaven. Through our Lord Jesus Christ.

—Prayer, *PS*, II, p. 350

Thoughts

- The hand for work, the heart for God.
  —Motto of Saint Zita

- A lazy servant ought not to be called pious; a person in our state who pretends to be pious without being essentially hardworking has nothing but false piety.
  —St. Zita

Resolutions

1 Be cheerful at home and at work to make the atmosphere pleasant.

2 Accept criticism without complaining.

3 Conduct yourself as a servant of your loved ones and colleagues, whatever your position, with discernment.

St. Peter Canisius

April 27

God speaks to us

Lo, I have set thee this day over the nations, and over the kingdoms, to root up, and pull down, and to waste, and to destroy, and to build, and to plant.

—Jeremias 1:10

Meditation

Peter Canisius (1521-1597) was born in Nijmegen (Netherlands). As a little boy, he learned to say Mass. At school, the behavior of certain students scandalized him. At the age of nineteen, he consecrated his virginity to God. Three years later, after attending an Ignatian retreat, he entered the Society of Jesus, a new religious order. Becoming a deacon in 1544, Peter was ordained a priest in 1546. Very quickly, he emerged as a man of learning, fundamentally good, and a great defender of papal authority. "Religious superior, educator, preacher, missionary, administrator, writer, theologian, diplomat, mediator, counselor of princes and of prelates, representing the Holy See, he assumed the various forms of Catholic action."[11] He was so zealous that he prevented the German-speaking world from going over entirely to the Lutheran heresy, hence his nickname "the hammer of heretics." He participated in the Council of Trent.

In his sermons, given to all the social classes, Peter struggled against religious ignorance and against the moral corruption that ensued. He was particularly interested in the formation and education of the clergy, and he endeavored to promote the building of Jesuit colleges. Peter was the spiritual master and organizer of the Society of Jesus in the Holy Roman Empire. His ministry extended from Holland to Italy, from Poland to Switzerland. He advised bishops and princes on questions concerning the reform of the Church and also the politics of the Church and the State. He was

---

[11] Benedictines, *Vies des saints,* Décembre (Letouzey, 1956), 599.

consulted by Saint Francis de Sales—then a young missionary—and the eminent Saint Charles Borromeo. He corresponded also with Cardinal Hosius, legate to the Council of Trent. We owe to Saint Peter Canisius a catechism with the tripartite form (creed, commandments, prayer and the sacraments) which we still find currently in many manuals. From 1572 to 1581, fifty-five editions followed one another, in nine languages. The holy Jesuit founded, lastly, Saint Michael's College, in Fribourg, Switzerland, where he passed the last seventeen years of his life. He died there very peacefully during the recitation of the Litany of the Saints.

Attributes and patronage

Saint Peter Canisius is depicted as a Jesuit, with his catechism in his hand. He is the secondary patron of Germany.

Prayer

O God, Who didst strengthen blessed Peter, Thy Confessor, by virtue and wisdom to defend the Catholic Faith: mercifully grant, that through his example and teaching the erring may return to the way of salvation and the faithful persevere in professing the truth. Through our Lord Jesus Christ. (Collect)

Thoughts

- We prefer to ruin, rather than maintain, what our elders had piously instituted…What is this widespread luxury, what are these pleasures that emasculate manly souls?'
 —St. Peter Canisius

- For my part, it is difficult for me to say how much the *Spiritual Exercises* [of Saint Ignatius] have changed my soul.

 —St. Peter Canisius, *E, t.* I, p. 77

Resolutions

1. Read a chapter of your catechism.
2. To examine your life and multiply your spiritual strengths, schedule a retreat during the year.
3. Become familiar with some of the errors of Protestantism and know how to refute them. If necessary, ask someone to enlighten you.

St. Paul of the Cross
April 28

God speaks to us

But we preach Christ crucified, unto the Jews indeed a stumbling block, and unto the Gentiles foolishness: But unto them that are called, both Jews and Greeks, Christ the power of God, and the wisdom of God.

—First Epistle of Saint Paul to the Corinthians 1:23-24

Meditation

Paul of the Cross (1694-1775), member of a family (Danei) with sixteen children, came from Castellazzo near Alessandria (Italy). While several of his brothers and sisters died at an early age, Giovanni Battista, his younger brother, would be his faithful companion. Around the age of twenty-five, Paul received from his bishop a black tunic provided with a heart surmounted with a cross carrying the inscription: "Passion of Jesus Christ."

He made a retreat of forty days in rudimentary physical conditions, where he made the resolution to combine an apostolic life with a life of great mortification. He began his career as a preacher with his brother Giovanni Battista, even while neither of them was a cleric. In 1721, they received all the orders in less than six months by virtue of an indult, and were ordained priests by Pope Benedict XIII. After completing their theological formation, they preached missions dealing with the last things and the Passion of Our Lord Jesus Christ. During the war between Austria, France, and Spain, Paul lived in Monte Argentario, an isolated mountain range in the Tuscan mountains, in Austrian territory. He preached to the soldiers of both armies without arousing suspicion. He brought many of them back to religious practice, which is all the more remarkable since he spoke neither French, nor Spanish, nor German.

After having rejected it on account of its strictness, the Holy See finally approved the Rule of the Passionists in 1741. To imitate Jesus' suffering and to draw the graces of conversion on sinners, the religious arise at midnight and practice numerous compulsory bodily mortifications. To the vows of poverty, chastity, and obedience, they join that of preaching the Passion of Jesus. After a very slow start for the Passionists, requests for admission poured in, so much so that upon the death of the founder in 1775, the congregation had fourteen houses called "Retreats," while the female branch had been born under the name of the Passionist nuns.

Attributes and Invocation

Saint Paul of the Cross is depicted in the habit of a Passionist, with the instruments of the Passion. He comes to the aid of candidates who must pass a foreign language examination.

Prayer

O Lord Jesus Christ, Who, for preaching the mystery of the cross didst endow Saint Paul with rare charity, and wast pleased that through him a new family should flourish in Thy Church: grant through his intercession for us, that we may ever bear in mind on earth the memory of Thy Passion and be accounted worthy to obtain its fruit in heaven. Who livest and reignest. (Collect)

Thoughts

- The persistent desire for the conversion of all sinners does not leave me, and I feel impelled to pray to God especially for this purpose in the desire I have to see him offended no longer.

  —St. Paul of the Cross, *D*, 15-18 December

- Live in peace at the feet of sweet Jesus, on His bare cross. In this holy rest in God, you will learn the science of the saints, and the blessed God will make you fit for apostolic ministries.

  —St. Paul of the Cross, *L3*, p. 702

Resolutions

1 Contemplate for ten minutes the five wounds of Jesus.

2 Read the narrative of the Passion in a Bible or in your missal.

3 Make a sacrifice while asking God for the conversion of a sinner with whom you are acquainted.

St. Peter of Verona

April 29

GOD SPEAKS TO US

Jesus said: Every one therefore that shall confess me before men, I will also confess him before my Father who is in heaven.
—Saint Matthew 10:32

MEDITATION

Peter of Verona (1206-1252) did not have the grace to be born into a Catholic family. His parents were Manicheans. They therefore believed in the existence of two principles at the origin of the world: a good god and an evil god. According to these heretics, this dualism was found in man. The soul was good and the body was evil, hence they accepted suicide, for example. Thus, this heresy was disastrous, not only on the religious level, but also for civil society. Peter was saved thanks to an uncle, his school teacher, who taught him the true religion. This man taught him that there is only one sovereign God who is all powerful, the Creator of heaven and earth. After this initial formation, Peter pursued his studies in Bologna. He preserved his innocence, thanks to the assistance of prayer, humility, and diligent work. At the age of sixteen years, he entered the Order of Preachers and received the habit of its founder, Saint Dominic. Extremely mortified during his novitiate, he ruined his health. Since God wanted religious, Peter recovered, thus enabling him to pronounce his vows and to pursue his studies. Once a priest, he instructed the faithful in the truths of the faith and attacked heresies, bringing about numerous conversions.

God favored him with the gift of miracles, but also with visions, which got him in trouble. He indeed received in his cell a visit from the virgins Catherine, Agnes, and Cecilia. This loosened gossiping tongues, and he was accused of attracting women to the convent. He accepted in silence the false accusations brought against him, and his superiors assigned him to the convent of Iesi, far from all ministry.

St. Peter of Verona

Far from complaining about it, he expected from God alone a sign of his innocence. In the end, the truth triumphed so clearly that Peter was restored to his original duties. God gave him a power over the elements of nature. One day, to confound heretics, during his sermon he took them at their word by cooling the atmosphere with the sudden appearance of a cloud in the heat of the day. Seeing the numerous conversions due to his prayers, his penitence, and his miracles, the heretics decided that he had to die. During a trip, he was struck on the head with an ax and a little after with the blow of a dagger in the heart which finished him. His assassin repented, entered the Dominicans as a cooperator brother, and there ended his days in penitence.

Prayer

Almighty God, we beseech Thee, that we may keep with all devotedness the faith of blessed Peter Thy Martyr, who for the spreading of that faith merited the palm of martyrdom. Through our Lord. (Collect)

Thoughts

- It truly shows great humility to let oneself to be condemned without being guilty, and it is a great imitation of the Lord who took all our sins upon Himself.
—St. Teresa of Avila, *PPJ*, June 25

- How many souls, on the day of judgment, will reproach us for not having replied with kindness and charity alone to their insults, because they would then be in Heaven!
—St. John Vianney, the Curé d'Ars, *PPJ*, September 17

Resolutions

1 Meditate on, then recite the Act of Faith with great attention.

2 Do not engage in any slander so as not to harm your neighbor's reputation.

3 Defend the Catholic faith calmly and carefully when someone denigrates it in front of you.

St. Catherine of Siena

April 30

God speaks to us

But it is good for me to adhere to my God, to put my hope in the Lord God.

—Psalm 72:28

Meditation

Last of twenty-four children, Saint Catherine of Siena (1347-1380) had a life marked by suffering. When she was twelve years old her parents wanted her to marry, but having made a vow of virginity at the age of seven, she emphatically refused, which provoked strained relations with them for several years. Finally, at nineteen years of age, she entered religious life with the Dominican tertiaries.

She slept and ate very little, contenting herself with the Holy Eucharist for several months. One day, when tempted by vanity and flirtation, she resisted with such a determination that the Blessed Virgin herself appeared to Catherine and put on her a magnificent dress covered with gold, pearls, and diamonds. Another time, the demon of impurity attacked her in turn. When she asked where was Jesus during this temptation, Our Lord said to her: "I am in you, for I never abandon those who do not abandon me." The saint also endured mystical trials. One Sunday, after Communion, she saw Our Lord crucified in front or her in the midst of a great light. Five rays radiated from his wounds and rested on her hands, his feet, and his side.

To help her in her trials, Catherine benefited from apparitions of saints and of Our Lord himself. Jesus smiled at her, blessed her, and even sometimes sang with her. Her love for God was manifested in her care for the good of the Church and for the salvation of souls. Thanks to her, Pope Gregory XI left Avignon to return to Rome (1378). She also did everything in her power to make peace between Florence, Siena, Naples, and the Holy See. One day, a man condemned to death, Nicholas Toldo, obstinately refused to confess. All he did was blaspheme; the saint went to see him. Touched by her words, he repented of his sins, and received absolution from a priest, then died pronouncing the name of Jesus. Having imitated so well her divine spouse on earth, Catherine, aged thirty-three years, rendered her soul to God.

Prayer

O God, Who didst grant to blessed Catherine—adorned with the special privileges of virginity and patience—to overcome the efforts of the evil spirits, and to remain steadfast in the love of Thy name, grant, we pray Thee, that following her example, by trampling underfoot the wickedness of the world, and by overcoming the attacks of all enemies, we may safely arrive at Thy glory. Through Jesus Christ. (Collect)

Thoughts

- Know, my daughter, that I am He who is, and that you are she who is not.

  —Jesus to Saint Catherine

- My mercy is incomparably greater than all the sins that all creatures can commit together: so it is the cruelest affront that anyone can do to Me to think that a creature's crime is greater than my goodness.

  —Jesus to Saint Catherine, *D*, II, p. 126

Resolutions

1. Pray the First Glorious Mystery for the Pope.
2. Avoid impurity by cutting off any future occasions of sin (such as a person, the internet, cell phone, etc.).
3. Make a resolution regarding flirtation (dress, perfume, hair style, etc.).

St. Marculf

May 1

GOD SPEAKS TO US

If any man will come after Me, let him deny himself, and take up his cross, and follow Me.

—St. Matthew 16:24

MEDITATION

In the Gospel, Jesus declared that the way of salvation is narrow and that few find it (Matthew 7:14). Marculf (d. ca. 558), having taken these words seriously, practiced the Christian virtues to a heroic degree.

Originally from Bayeux in Normandy, he was born into a family illustrious for its nobility and its conduct. From his boyhood, he manifested beautiful dispositions of piety, mortification, and charity towards the poor. As a young man, he lost his parents and sold his patrimony for the poor. The sacrifice of material goods was only the prelude to the way of perfection. Indeed, he hastened to leave the world to devote himself totally to God, placing himself under the leadership of Saint Possessor, Bishop of Coutances. The holy bishop ordained him a priest and sent him to preach in the diocese, but soon, when Marculf felt a great desire to withdraw from the world to bury himself in the solitude of a cloister, an angel appeared to him and urged him to go find King Childebert I to ask him to build a monastery in the land of Nanteuil, in the Diocese of Coutances (Normandie). He obeyed the celestial voice and found several companions to live under his direction. In his retreat, he became a living image of Our Lord. One day, Marculf was inspired to imitate Christ in His forty–day fast by retiring to a desert island. There, in the form of a shameless creature claiming to be the victim of a shipwreck, Satan tempted Marculf by asking him for shelter and a piece of bread. Discovering the trap, the saint, by a simple sign of the cross, put the enemy to flight. During this time of penitence, he took for his nourishment only a little barley bread and raw herbs three times a week, and slept on a hard rock. On his return to his monastery at Easter, he edified his brothers by his faithfulness to prayer and to penitence for the rest of his days. After exhorting them to struggle generously against the traps of the devil, Marculf lifted his eyes and hands towards heaven and rendered his soul to God.

Attributes, invocation, and patronage

Saint Marculf is clothed as an abbot, and is accompanied by a sick man who solicits the saint's healing. He is invoked for diseases of the skin. He is the patron of apothecaries.

Prayer

O God of mercy and of all consolation, by the merits and the powerful intercession of Saint Marculf, abbot and confessor, grant us peace and salvation of soul and body, so that we may live according to Thy commandments and do always what is pleasing to Thee. Through Jesus Christ. (Collect)

Thoughts

- Have a heart full of compassion for the poor, and help them with love, as much as you can, because they have the name of Jesus Christ engraved on their foreheads.
—St. Paul of the Cross, *PPJ*, September 3

- Carefully avoid any danger of offending not only against purity, but even against the smallest rules of modesty.

—St. Paul of the Cross, *PPJ*, July 3

Resolutions

1 Take ten minutes in the day to recollect yourself in the presence of God in a church or in your room.

2 Be modest in your dress and your behavior so as to protect the beautiful virtue of purity in yourself and in others.

3 Do not omit your contributions to the Church in order to support the devoted and faithful clergy.

St. Athanasius

May 2

GOD SPEAKS TO US

In all things we suffer tribulation, but are not distressed; we are straitened, but are not destitute; We suffer persecution, but are not forsaken; we are cast down, but we perish not.
—Second Epistle to the Corinthians 4:8-9

MEDITATION

Athanasius (ca. 295-373) was born in Alexandria (Egypt) of Christian parents. After having him instructed in the secular sciences, they confided him to Saint Alexander. Athanasius put all his effort into learning the things of God, and he did it so well that later he gave the impression of knowing Holy Scripture by memory. Reading with much interest the writings of the ancient doctors of the Church, he strengthened his Catholic spirit, and discovered the true sense of the Scriptures and of the mystery of the Incarnation, whose intrepid defender he would soon become. At the death of Alexander, Patriarch of Alexandria, Athanasius was only a simple deacon, but he found himself burdened with the responsibility for a large see. From the day of his election on, his strong temperament flourished: one could not find a man more resolute or nobly inflexible. During the forty-six years of his episcopate, he passed five in exile on account of his firmness in defending the faith. Absolutely convinced that his cause was that of the truth, that God would triumph sooner or later, he never wavered or compromised on the substance of the debate that pitted him against the Arians. Even in the worst moments of the struggle, he never despaired, nor doubted the final victory, but he didn't wait for it with his hands folded. He did everything he could humanly do to ensure it.

His martyr's soul did not keep him from defending himself against the attacks and slander to which he was subjected; when pursued and hunted down, he fled. Combining the flexibility of his procedures with the firmness of his convictions, he knew how to stall, hold back his overzealous friends, and speak to the wavering in the language of peacemaking. He was a true leader whose authority was never contested. Faith with integrity found in him its defender to the point where sometimes he remained almost its sole guardian. He had to battle against the Roman Empire and its agents, the councils, and the episcopacy. His last years of his life were the only peaceful ones. It was time for him to receive the promised wages of a good and faithful servant, he who had participated so valiantly in the victory of Christian doctrine over the Arian heresy, becoming thus the prototype of integral orthodoxy. Among his writings, we can cite the *Discourse against the Gentiles* and the *Discourse on the Incarnation of the Word; The Apology against the Arians; and The Apology to the Emperor Constantius.*

Attributes and invocation

Saint Athanasius is depicted as an Eastern bishop, with a book in his hand. He is invoked against headaches.

Prayer

On this feast day of blessed Athanasius, Thy Confessor and Bishop, hear our prayers to Thee, O Lord, and since he gave Thee such worthy service, be mindful of his merits and blot out all our sins. Through our Lord. (Collect)

Thoughts

- Virginity is like a closed garden, which is not trodden on by anyone except its gardener.
 —St. Athanasius, *V,* p. 225

- You fast by abstaining from food and nourishment, you keep your belly empty; only do not fill yourself with sins by meditating evil things against your neighbor or by scorning your mother or by becoming angry.
 —St. Athanasius, *V,* p. 227

Resolutions

1. Recite the Creed with all care.
2. Read a chapter of doctrine to be able to defend the Catholic faith, and ask a priest to explain, if necessary.
3. Defend the Catholic faith when it is attacked.

Finding of the Holy Cross

May 3

God speaks to us

But God forbid that I should glory, save in the cross of our Lord Jesus Christ; by whom the world is crucified to me, and I to the world.

—Galatians 6:14

Meditation

The Church celebrates today the finding of the Cross (328), that is, the discovery of the Cross of Our Lord by Saint Helena. Indeed, the mother of Emperor Constantine, shortly before her death, traveled to the Holy Places and had excavations done at the supposed location of Calvary, the location where a temple to Venus had been built. There she found three crosses, the nails which had pierced the hands and feet of the Savior, and the inscription which Pilate had had placed above His head. In order to determine whether this was the cross of Jesus, the Bishop of Jerusalem suggested that the three crosses be placed in contact with a sick woman. While the approach of the first two crosses had produced no effect on the sick woman, as soon as the third cross touched her, she was instantly healed. A second miracle came soon to confirm the fact. A dead person who was being buried was resurrected immediately after coming into contact with the sacred wood. To these miracles, we must add the multiplication of fragments over the centuries. As St. Paulinus of Nola says, "this divine cross, while allowing itself to be reduced to fragments, to satisfy the desire of countless faithful, is not thereby diminished. Thus, it is divisible in favor of those to whom it is distributed, and remains entire to the devotion of those who adore it."[12] Today, the largest fragment of the Cross is found in Rome in the Basilica of Holy Cross of Jerusalem.

We honor the cross of Our Lord inasmuch as it was the instrument of our salvation. We will venerate it, for by the cross Our Lord vanquished Satan, the enemy of our souls. Jesus willed to carry it so that we might merit heaven, and to show us the way to join Him one day in blessed eternity.

O my Jesus, with a heart full of adoration and love, I turn to Your holy Cross. I want to embrace it with devotion, and also carry it in my daily life. Strengthen me, support me, guide me!

Prayer

O God, Who didst cause that the Cross of our salvation should in most honorable wise be found again, and Who didst manifest thereby the marvelous efficacy of Thy sufferings, mercifully grant that by the Ransom which Thou didst pay upon that tree of life we may finally attain unto life eternal. Who livest and reignest. (Collect)

Thoughts

- Take in your hands a crucifix and, in a slow meditation, ask yourself who it is hanging on the cross, what is the nature of His sacrifice, what is the intensity of His sorrows.

    —Msgr. de Llobet, *LP*, 1933

- Resignation in trial, patience in adversity, courage in the performance of duty, perseverance in effort, holy enthusiasm in heroism: a whole gamut of feelings which, according to circumstances, the Cross inspires in the heart of a Christian.

    —Msgr. de Llobet, *LP*, 1933

---

[12] *Letter* XXXI to Sulpicius Severus, PL, t. LXI, col. 326.

Resolutions

1. Contemplate Jesus on the cross for ten minutes, taking as support the first thought of this day.
2. Make the sign of the cross when passing by a wayside cross.
3. Have a beautiful crucifix in your home and often look with love while thinking about the price of our salvation.

St. Monica

May 4

God speaks to us

They that sow in tears shall reap in joy.

—Psalm 125:5

Meditation

The greatest grace that Our Lord can give to a child is to give him parents according to His Divine Heart. This grace of choice Monica (332-387) received at her birth in Carthage (Tunisia). Her parents communicated to her the spirit of prayer and penitence, dispositions which could be given only to a strong and holy soul. At the age of twenty-two, for lack of clear-sightedness or through weakness, they gave her hand in marriage to a certain Patricius, a man of noble blood, but a pagan. He combined a choleric temperament with very lax morals. Monica strove through exemplary behavior and ardent prayer to touch his heart. She strove to win him over by her virtues; she constantly proved to be humble, gentle, patient, devoted, and she suffered her martyrdom without complaining, weeping only in secret. Since she was always attentive to please him on all points that her Christian conscience did not disapprove of, Patricius could never fault her. He ended up by converting after twenty-seven years of marriage.

Meanwhile, however, Monica had to face another trial. Although shortly after her marriage she experienced the joys of motherhood by bringing three children into the world, Augustine, the eldest, "gave her a hard time." During his childhood, Augustine received from his mother the great principles of the faith, but, at around the age of sixteen, he started to develop bad instincts; being drawn to the world, he slid lamentably down the slope of vice. His father's culpable carelessness, combined with dangerous reading and even more dangerous attendance at licentious theaters, did their destructive work. During these years, Saint Monica's fervent prayers and suppliant tears had no tangible effect on her unfaithful son. At the death of her husband, God finally responded to her wait. Jesus rekindled the faith of her child to grace through the channel of Saint Ambrose, Bishop of Milan. Her task was accomplished: she could now die. A little later, she fell sick and rendered her soul to God the ninth day of her illness, in Ostia (Italy).

Attributes, invocation, and patronage

Saint Monica is depicted as a widow. She is invoked for the education of children, and she is the patron of widows.

Prayer

O God, Comforter of the sorrowful and salvation of them that hope in Thee, Who didst mercifully receive the devoted tears of blessed Monica for the conversion of her son Augustine: enable us through their joint intercession to bewail our sins and to find merciful grace from Thee. Through our Lord. (Collect)

Thoughts

- God has heard me abundantly, [Augustine], since I now see you despising the happiness of the earth to dedicate yourself to his service. What am I still doing here?
—St. Monica to Saint Augustine

- I ask only one thing: remember me [after my death] before the altar of the Lord, wherever you may be.
—St. Monica to Saint Augustine

Resolutions

1 Pray the Fifth Joyful Mystery to implore from God the conversion of a young delinquent.

2 Have a Mass celebrated for your deceased parents.

3 Show great determination in the education of your children, to lead them to good things, and add to this the example of Christian virtues.

St. Pius V

May 5

God speaks to us

The Lord raises up the needy from the earth... That He may place him with princes, with the princes of his people.
—Psalm 112:7-8

Meditation

Michele Ghislieri (1504-1572) was a member of an old ruined family from Bosco, near Alessandria (Italy). At twelve years of age he received formation from the Dominicans, who were edified by his intelligence and piety. Ordained a priest in 1528, he was charged with the instruction of the friars. Ghislieri studied the errors of the Protestants, who were then setting Europe ablaze. Appointed Inquisitor of the Faith, he burned their books that were poisoning souls. Having become Commissary General of the Holy Office (1551), Ghislieri proved to be firm against error, while seeking to win over heretics through gentleness and reflection. He pardoned, then converted, Sixtus of Siena, a famous Jew; the latter soon became a Dominican and devoted the rest of his life to the conversion of the Jews. A bishop, then a cardinal, Michele Ghislieri was finally elected pope in 1564, taking the name of Pius V.

Pius V revised the Roman Missal to re-establish the unity of the liturgy in the Western Church. One of his major worries was the extension of the Muslim conquests. After having failed to take Malta, the Muslims went to Cyprus in 1570; the town of Famagusta surrendered after eleven months of siege. Bragadino, one of the Catholic leaders, endured horrible tortures at the orders of Mustapha, the Turkish general. In Nicosia, the Muslims cut the throats of 20,000 victims, reserving two thousand slaves for themselves. The Pope, who was closely following these horrors, saw no other solution than to wage a great battle against them to protect Europe. It was led by Don John of Austria, son of Charles V, at Lepanto. The Turkish fleet had more than three hundred vessels, while the Catholics had only 209 ships at their disposal. The Pope ordered a three-day fast and a rosary crusade; all the sailors made their confession and received Holy Communion. On October 7, 1571, during the battle, the Muslims were seized with terror. They lost more than two hundred vessels and thirty thousand men. This victory was a mortal blow delivered to the naval power of the Turks. Pius V was called back to God the following year.

Attributes

Saint Pius V is depicted with a rosary or kissing a crucifix.

Prayer

O God, Who for the overthrow of the enemies of Thy Church and for the restoration of divine worship didst vouchsafe to choose blessed Pius as Supreme Pontiff: grant that we may be defended by his patronage and so cleave to Thy service, that overcoming all the wiles of our enemies, we may rejoice in perpetual peace. Through our Lord. (Collect)

Thoughts

- Our heart and our strength, all our thoughts are oriented towards this goal: to guard in its purity the [liturgical] worship celebrated by the Holy Roman Church.
—St. Pius V

- The Holy Eucharist is the center of all Catholic worship—it is her life, her royalty, her heaven—we say it plainly—it is Jesus Christ, [...] God with us, in our midst, for us.
—St. Peter-Julian Eymard, *PPJ*, January 4

Resolutions

1 Pray a rosary to ask for the conversion of the Muslims.

2 Attend Mass devoutly and receive Holy Communion.

3 Learn from someone competent which *suras* of the Koran are opposed the dogma of the Trinity.

St. Dominic Savio

May 6

GOD SPEAKS TO US

Being made perfect in a short space, he fulfilled a long time: For his soul pleased God: therefore he hastened to bring him out of the midst of iniquities.

—Wisdom 4:13-14

MEDITATION

The oldest of nine children, Dominic Savio (1842-1857) was born in Piedmont (Italy).

From a very young age, he showed signs of sanctity. Sweet, pious, obedient, he was a model child. He showed already the presence in him of the gifts of the Holy Ghost, and notably the gift of wisdom, which enabled him to taste the heavenly realities and to live an orderly life.

To increase the practice of the virtues, he had recourse to Marian devotion. Saint John Bosco noticed this during the three years that Saint Dominic lived in his company. He had acquired this devotion in his family, where they prayed the *Angelus* and the rosary together. Having the grace to receive Holy Communion from the age of seven on, he wrote: "My friends will be Jesus and Mary." Two months after his entrance into Don Bosco's school, on December 8, 1854, the day on which the dogma of the Immaculate Conception was proclaimed, he renewed at the altar of the Virgin his resolutions from First Communion, adding these words: "O Mary, I give you my heart. May it always be yours. O Jesus, O Mary, never stop being my friends. Please let me die rather than having the misfortune of committing sin." His piety reached its peak during the month of Mary. He received Communion and urged his friends to do the same to honor her who gave Jesus to the world. The year before his death, having no money to contribute to adorn the month of Mary, he sold the books that he had won for his good conduct and excellent grades, since he was always first in his class. So as never to offend the Blessed Virgin, he watched over the purity of his eyes. To a friend who was astonished by his custody of the eyes when he went out on the street, he responded: "I want to guard my eyes the better to see my Heavenly Mother when I go to paradise." He also made sure to be an example for his comrades in order to encourage them to do good. While some of them mocked and mistreated him, others followed him in his apostolic movement, which he placed under the patronage of the Immaculate Conception.

At the end of his short life, after having prayed the prayers for the dying with his father, he said to him: "Farewell, dear Papa. Farewell! Oh! What I see is so beautiful…" then he rendered his beautiful soul to God on the evening of March 9, 1857.

Patronage

Saint Dominic is patron of youth and of purity.

Prayer

O God, Who by Saint Dominic, hast given to young people an admirable example of piety and purity, grant us in Thy mercy that, by his intercession and his example, we may be capable of serving Thee with a chaste body and a pure heart. Through our Lord. (Collect)

Thoughts

- What I ask of you is that you make me a saint.
  —St. Dominic Savio to Saint John Bosco

- May God, my dear Friend, help us to be holy and to become saints quickly!
  —St. Dominic Savio to a friend

Resolutions

1 Pray the Litany of the Blessed Virgin. (See Appendix.)

2 Keep watch over the purity of your eyes in the street and during screen time.

3 Ask God for the grace to die rather than to commit a single mortal sin, and for that purpose, flee the near occasions of sin.

St. Stanislaus, Bishop

May 7

GOD SPEAKS TO US

And fear ye not them that kill the body, and are not able to kill the soul: but rather fear Him that can destroy both soul and body in hell.

—Matthew 10:28

MEDITATION

Stanislaus (1030-1079) was born near Krakow (Poland), to very virtuous parents. He began his university studies in Poland and continued them in Paris for seven years. Upon his return to his homeland, after the death of his parents, he inherited a considerable fortune and hastened to distribute it to the poor. Ordained a priest by the Bishop of Krakow, he was named a canon of the cathedral. He edified the whole chapter by his conduct and instituted a reform of morals. When the Bishop died, Stanislaus was chosen to occupy his see, but he agreed to succeed him only after Pope Alexander II intervened. Once installed as Bishop, he kept his hair shirt and showed great charity to the poor.

Poland was ruled by Boleslaus II, a degenerate prince. Stanislaus did not hesitate to admonish him severely and managed for a time to make him repent. But very quickly Boleslaus resumed his scandalous life. He forcefully abducted the wife of a lord, a woman named Christine who was remarkable for her virtue and beauty. All of Poland was scandalized by Boleslaus' behavior: nevertheless, several bishops did not dare to intervene for fear of reprisals, knowing his violence. Stanislaus alone confronted the king once again and begged him to change his conduct, under pain of excommunication. The monarch, furious, decided to take revenge as soon as an opportunity arose. One day Stanislaus purchased some land from a man named Peter. Everything was done legally, but the holy bishop was content to make this purchase in front of witnesses without leaving a written record. After the death of the seller, the King sought out the nephews of the deceased and convinced them to claim back from Stanislaus the land that had belonged to their uncle, as if it were stolen property. They gave in to the leader's insistence. Stanislaus was then summoned before an assembly of judges with the King presiding. The enemies of Stanislaus pretended that he had usurped the land and the saint was on the brink of being condemned. Stanislaus fasted and prayed for three days, then ordered the deceased former owner to come out of his tomb and appear in court. The man, who had been dead for three years, instantly got up, went to court, declared that Stanislaus had purchased the land according to the rules of the trade, then went back to his tomb. The King was impressed and changed his behavior for a while, but returned to his disorders and ended up killing the holy Bishop while he was celebrating Mass.

Patronage

Saint Stanislaus is one of the patrons of Poland.

Prayer

O God, for Whose honor the glorious Bishop Stanislaus fell beneath the swords of wicked men: grant, we beseech Thee, that all who implore his aid may obtain the wholesome fulfillment of their prayers. Through Jesus Christ. (Collect)

Thoughts

- The devil is a liar and the father of lies.

—John 8 :44

- Stand therefore, having your loins girt about with truth, and having on the breastplate of justice,

—Ephesians 6 :14

Resolutions

1 Pray to God that our bishops will be courageous in their mission as defenders of the social reign of Christ the King.

2 Avoid lying at all costs.

3 Do not make false statements or defraud in sales.

The Apparition of Saint Michael

May 8

GOD SPEAKS TO US

And there was a great battle in heaven, Michael and his angels fought with the dragon, and the dragon fought and his angels: And they prevailed not, neither was their place found any more in heaven.

—Apocalypse 12:7-8

MEDITATION

The devils attempt to make men turn away from God, hate Him, and lose their souls so as to join them in hell. Every Christian must struggle against them and courageously wage the battle against these beings who dominate by their spiritual nature. In this battle, he is supported by the good angels, headed by Saint Michael. The great Archangel, head of the celestial army, is the model of the worship due to God and of carrying out God's orders. Church history teaches us that as early as the first half of the fourth century, Pope Sylvester I dedicated a shrine in Sabina to him. In the following century, during the pontificate of Saint Leo the Great, the feast of Saint Michael was celebrated in Rome, and on May 8, 492, he appeared on Mount Gargano. In the kingdom of Naples, near Manfredonia, a rich man named Gargan was grazing his herds when one of his bulls disappeared into the mountain. After several days of fruitless searching, he ended up finding the bull in a cavern. Someone then shot an arrow at the bull, which went back to wound the shooter. The companions of the unfortunate archer, who were witnesses to this mysterious incident, went to find the local bishop who, after three days of prayer and penance, was blessed with an appearance by the great Archangel. Saint Michael informed him that he wanted a sanctuary to be built in this place, under his name and in honor of all the angels. The Bishop then went to the place with all his clergy and observed that the cavern was arranged in the form of a church. They built a sanctuary there, where God worked several miracles. The place has since received the name of Monte Sant'Angelo (Holy Angel Mountain). In 1002, according to Saint Peter Damian, Emperor Otto III had to go there barefoot, performing a penance given by Saint Romuald for having put Senator Crescentius to death, contrary to Otto's promise. Saint Michael appeared again, to Pope Saint Gregory the Great, in Rome; and in 708 to Saint Aubert, Bishop of Avranches, to ask him to build a place of worship dedicated to him, on Mount Tombe, which today bears his name.

Saint Michael the Archangel, we trust in you: enlighten us, protect us, save us.

Attributes and Patronage

Saint Michael is depicted as a handsome young man with his raised foot on the head of a dragon which he pierces with a lance. Michael is the patron of parachutists.

Prayer

Saint Michael the Archangel, defend us in battle: that we may not perish in the dreadful judgment.
—Alleluia of the Mass for Saint Michael

Thoughts

- Today my whole heart sings the challenge of Michael: "Who is like God?…"
    —Elizabeth of the Trinity, *PPJ*, September 29

- Saint Michael, although prince of the heavenly host, is most zealous in paying all kinds of homage to God; Michael is always waiting to have the honor of going, at God's word, to rescue one of his servants.'
    —St. Augustine, v, p. 41

Resolutions

1 Read the prayer to Saint Michael in the Appendix.

2 Obtain a beautiful image of Saint Michael and pray to him in the temptations associated in particular to the reckless use of the internet, radio, and telephone.

3 Dare to talk about the devil, whose greatest trick is to make people believe that he does not exist.

St. Gregory of Nazianzus

May 9

GOD SPEAKS TO US

And he shall direct his counsel, and his knowledge, and in His secrets shall he meditate.

—Epistle: Ecclesiasticus 39:10

MEDITATION

Gregory Nazianzen (328-389) was the son of Saint Nonna. His father, converted by his wife, later became Saint Gregory the Elder, Bishop of Nazianzus, in Cappadocia (Turkey); the son would succeed his father in this office. He recounted that one day he saw in a dream two virgins who invited him to follow them on the way of perfection. "We are chastity and purity," they added, "and we are both companions of Jesus Christ and the friends of those who preserve virginity to lead a heavenly life." Immediately Gregory made the decision to renounce definitively the joys of marriage and to devote himself to study with the utmost care. He dedicated himself to it in Athens, where he met Saint Basil, with whom he formed a great friendship that he would maintain his whole life.

During these years, Gregory was torn between the desire to lead a hidden life with Basil and the desire to comply with his father's expectations by taking part in the government of the Church through the exercise of his priestly ministry. In 372 he was consecrated a bishop by his friend Basil, who had become Bishop of Caesarea.

Shortly afterward, Gregory's parents died; he then retired to Seleucia. Basil in turn died in 379, and Gregory subsequently became the Patriarch of Constantinople. There he revealed his talent as a speaker in his discourses on the Holy Trinity, which earned him the nickname of *Theologian*. The efficacy of his words came from his life of renunciation and prayer. At each Mass, he offered himself to God in oblation with the Divine Victim on the altar of sacrifice. But soon, a tempest was brewing against him. The devil stirred up Gregory's enemies, and he was finally dismissed from his rank of Patriarch by a council, in favor of a certain Paulinus of Antioch. Gregory, who still had a great desire for a solitary life, wanted nothing else. Nonetheless, in a moving discourse he left his faithful with these words: "My dear children, guard the deposit of faith; remember the stones you threw at me while I was trying to plant it in your hearts!"

He dedicated the final years of his life to prayer, fasting, and the writing of his works.

Saint Gregory, I want to offer myself at each Mass, like you, in oblation with Jesus the victim, so as finally to submit constantly to the will of God.

Prayer

O God, who hast given blessed Gregory to Thy people as a minister of eternal salvation: grant, we beseech Thee, that we, who have had him for our teacher on earth, may deserve to have him for our advocate in heaven. Through our Lord,
—Collect

Thoughts

- God desires to be desired; He thirsts for men to have thirst for Him.

    —St. Gregory, *Discourse,* §60

- No one can truly approach the great God, him who is our pontiff and our victim, unless he himself is a living and holy victim, unless he offers himself in perpetual sacrifice.

    —St. Gregory, *2nd Discourse,* §95

Resolutions

1 Recite three times with devotion, the prayer "Glory be to the Father and to the Son and to the Holy Ghost…" to honor the Three Divine Persons.

2 In order to intensify your life of union with God, set aside fifteen minutes today to pray with fervor.

3 Think about offering yourself with Jesus at the altar at the moment when the priest puts a drop of water in the chalice at the offertory.

St. Solange

May 10

GOD SPEAKS TO US

For the foolishness of God is wiser than men; and the weakness of God is stronger than men.

—I Corinthians 1:25

MEDITATION

Solange (d. 880) was born near Bourges into a family of honest laborers. Her parents gave her a hatred for mortal sin and of all that could offend God. From the age of seven, she consecrated her virginity to the Divine Master, not wanting to have any spouse other than Jesus Christ. She sensed that virginity would permit her to live perpetually in peace and to experience an interior joy much greater than what she would have if she married, but she also realized that in order to preserve her virginity, it was not enough for her to commit herself by a vow, she must protect it through prayer, penance, and a life as far away from the world as possible. And so she asked her parents whether she could look after the flocks on the farm. Country life greatly facilitated the elevation of her soul towards God. While the contemplation of nature made her discover the beauty of God, His wisdom, goodness, and power, Solange also benefited from heavenly visions; she frequently found herself in ecstasy. Also, she received the power to command a storm, to drive away with a simple sign of her will the animals that tried to harm her flock. She healed numerous sick persons and put devils to flight.

Divine grace further ennobled Solange's beauty and charm, and Dynaste, the son of the regional governor, conceived an intense passion for her. He promised to make her the mistress of his possessions if she consented to marry him. But Solange, strengthened interiorly by the Holy Ghost, emphatically refused his proposal, telling him that she had dedicated herself to Jesus Christ forever. The young man, furious at seeing his advances scorned, then used force with her and abducted her on his horse. When crossing a stream, Solange managed to escape from his hands but he caught her again, drew his sword, and cut off her head. It was then that by a marvelous miracle the lips of the saint repeated three times the name of Jesus. Moreover, her historian reports that she then took her head in her hands and carried it to the place where later there would be built a sanctuary in her honor.

Attributes and patronage

Saint Solange is depicted watching her sheep, with a star above her head. She is the patroness of Berry.

Prayer

Lord Jesus Christ, Thou Who hast established Thy dwelling in a chaste heart, grant to us who celebrate with a fervent homage the merits of blessed Solange, Thy virgin and martyr, to follow her example by the integrity of our faith and of our life. Thou Who livest and reignest… (Collect)

Thoughts

- A pure soul is close to God as an infant is close to its mother.
—St. John Vianney, the Curé of Ars, *PPJ*, December 28

- Assign the shares justly: keep what is yours, that is, a terrible nothingness, capable of bringing forth all possible evils, and leave to God what is His, that is, everything good.
—St. Paul of the Cross, *PPJ*, July 11

Resolutions

1 Pray the Fourth Joyful Mystery in asking the Blessed Virgin for the virtue of purity.

2 Avoid drawing attention to yourself by flirtatiousness or in conversations so as to acquire humility.

3 Respect nature and see in her the work of God, with forgetting the fact that it shares today in our sinful state.

St. Gengulphus

May 11

God speaks to us

For this is thankworthy, if for conscience towards God, a man endure sorrows, suffering wrongfully.

—I Peter 2:19

Meditation

Too often we are apt to find an excuse in the family, social, or ecclesiastical setting in which we live to think that virtue is impractical or at least to believe that holiness beyond our reach. The rich man declares that he is too absorbed in his possessions, the poor man—that he is too preoccupied by cares about money; the sick person says that he no longer has the strength to pray, and the person in good health—that he doesn't have the time. In reality, everything that happens to us in our life is sent to us by Providence for our salvation. Therefore, we should use it for our sanctification following the example of Saint Gengulph (d. 760). Born into a rich and profoundly Christian family of the Diocese of Langres, he was orphaned at the age of eighteen by the loss of both his father and mother; Gengulph then inherited great wealth. Far from squandering it on frivolities, though, he used it to build churches and to care for the poor. He did not use the loss of his parents as an excuse to liberate himself from all authority, but on the contrary he strove to live more in the presence of God.

He enlisted in the army of Pepin the Short—son of Charles Martel and father of Charlemagne—as an officer. There Gengulph did not let himself to be corrupted by the surrounding environment, which was not conducive to virtue, but preserved more than ever—his biographer tells us—his ideal of serving God and the King.

Finally, he overcame valiantly the saddest trial of his life. His wife, who was of the same social rank as he but did not have the same degree of virtue, was leading a double life. As a Christian, Gengulph knew that he was united with her forever for better or for worse. And so he did not take advantage of his wife's infidelity to imitate her. He loved her faithfully; he had compassion for the unfaithful woman: he wanted to save her soul. Frightened at the prospect of seeing her damn herself, he urged his wife to do penance and promised to forgive her if she would agree to return to him, but it was wasted effort. And so he saw no other solution than to leave his marital home and to retire to one of his lands, near Avallon. That was where his wife's lover killed him by surprise by running him through with a sword.

Attributes and patronage

Saint Gengulph, depicted as a lord, with a dog, a falcon, or even a horse, is invoked by unhappily married people.

Prayer

Grant, almighty God, to us who celebrate the birth into heaven of blessed Gengulph, Thy martyr, the grace to be, by his intercession, strengthened in the love of Thy name. Through Jesus Christ. (Collect)

Thoughts

- The divine will is a balm which heals all sorrows; we must caress it and love it in adversity as in prosperity.
  —St. Paul of the Cross, *PPJ*, July 19

- Never look at the instrumental cause of your trials, but imagine that Jesus Christ is presenting them to you with his own hand.
  —St. Paul of the Cross, *PPJ*, July 17

Resolutions

1. Pray the Second Joyful Mystery that married people may give one another mutual support in their spiritual life.

2. Caution young people not to get involved romantically with someone they would be unwilling or unable to marry, so as to avoid inextricable situations.

3. Forgive each other for mistakes committed as a couple, and renew your vows of fidelity with the help of Saint Gengulph.

St. Pancras

May 12

God speaks to us

But the just that is dead, condemneth the wicked that are living, and youth soon ended, the long life of the unjust.
—Wisdom 4:16

Meditation

It is beautiful to see an adolescent desire at all costs to remain faithful to the promises of his baptism and try constantly to live up to the certitudes of the faith. However, it is still more edifying to meet a young man who, faced with tyrants, preferred to die rather than renounce his faith. He is worthy of admiration, he who said to his executioners: "You can make me suffer and die, but I will stay faithful to Jesus Christ, who has proved His love for me in dying for me on the cross." Such was the heroism of Saint Pancras (d. 304).

At the beginning of the fourth century, after 250 years of persecution, the establishment of the Christian religion was such in the Roman Empire that one could hope to see it enjoy full freedom. It had indeed triumphed over nine terrible persecutions. Three times in twenty-five years, the Roman emperors had sought to drown it in blood. However, despite this bloodshed, God permitted the Church to suffer yet another final trial. Under Diocletian it was the bloodiest and longest of the persecutions. It lasted ten years, which earned it the epithet "era of martyrs." During this period Pancras, an orphan from Phrygia (Asia Minor), was growing up. Since the death of his parents, he had lived under the tutelage of his uncle Denis. In 304, at the age of fourteen, he went with him to Rome, and both received Baptism there after instructions in the mysteries of the Catholic faith. One day the Emperor, learning of Pancras' uncle Denis, summoned Pancras to his palace. An old friend of his father, Diocletian made Pancras the most seductive promises, treating him with kindness and promising him honors, riches, pleasures, on the condition that he abandon the Christian faith and serve his ancestral gods. Pancras very serenely retorted: "I am astonished that you command me to have esteem for your gods while you would inflict the death penalty on any slaves who led such a depraved life as theirs." Furious at this response, Diocletian ordered him tortured, then sentenced him to be decapitated.

Saint Pancras, look benevolently upon us, so that we may not let ourselves be corrupted by flattery and may never abandon our religious practice for fear of displeasing the world.

Attributes, Invocation, and Patronage

Saint Pancras is depicted under the form of a young man, having for an optional attribute the sword of his martyrdom. He is the protector of olive trees and the patron of children.

Prayer

O Lord, we beseech Thee, may the happy solemnity of Thy Martyr Pancras ever defend us from evil and render us more worthy to serve Thee. Through our Lord. (Collect)

Thoughts

- Drink sweetly from the chalice that Jesus Christ himself offers you; although it is bitter to the palate, it is sweet to the heart.

  —St. Paul of the Cross, *PPJ*, August 17

- God has suffered so much for me: Is it too much for me to do something for his love?

  —St. Paul of the Cross, *PPJ*, August 27

Resolutions

1 Recite a *Magnificat* in thanksgiving for your Baptism.

2 Witness to the joy of being Catholic the next time the opportunity arises.

3 Help adolescents to make good use of their liberty by showing them the good fruits that they will gather from doing so.

St. Robert Bellarmine

May 13

God speaks to us

Wherefore I wished, and understanding was given me: and I called upon God, and the spirit of wisdom came upon me.
—Wisdom 7:7

Meditation

Robert Bellarmine (1542-1621) was born in Montepulciano, in Tuscany, into a family which eventually had twelve children. Early in life he distinguished himself by his virtue and his aptitude for studies. At the age of eighteen, he entered the Jesuits. He followed the classic *cursus*: novitiate, philosophical studies, then theological studies. The University of Louvain was where he studied theology at the request of his superior, Saint Francis Borgia. After his priestly ordination in 1569, he taught Thomistic theology there for seven years. From there, he then went to Rome, where the General of the Order entrusted to him the chair of controversy [apologetics] (1576-1588). The publication of his course resulted in a three-volume book entitled *Controversies*. They discuss God, Jesus Christ, the Church, the sacraments, and grace. This masterpiece made him the great defender of Christian doctrine against the heretics, and especially against the writings of Luther and Calvin.

Given the power of his work and the extent of his knowledge, he also dealt with other historical, biblical, legal subjects, etc. In particular, he wrote a commentary on the psalms. In 1588, he was appointed spiritual director at the Roman College for four years. He counted among his directees Saint Aloysius Gonzaga, then Saint John Berchmans. Subsequently he was named director of this same institution for a two-year term before going to Naples, where he became Provincial of his Order. He governed it with prudence and wisdom.

Then Rome called him: there, as a member of the Roman Curia, Theologian of the Holy Office during the Galileo affair, member of the Commission for the revision of the Vulgate, Bellarmine was created cardinal and counselor to the Pope before being named archbishop of Capua; he occupied this see for three years. He especially tackled the reform of the clergy and showed his charity by his care for the poor. Later he returned to Rome at the request of the newly elected Paul V. As Prefect of the Congregation of Rites, he dealt with the canonization of Raymond of Penyafort, Frances of Rome, and Charles Borromeo, Bishop of Milan.

Having arrived at the end of his life, aged seventy-nine years, he rendered his soul to God, filled with merits, after reciting the *Credo*. His body reposes in Rome in the Church of Saint Ignatius.

Prayer

O God, Who didst adorn blessed Robert, Thy Bishop and Doctor, with wondrous learning and virtue that he might lay bare the snares of error and maintain the rights of the Apostolic See, grant by his merits and intercession that we may grow in love of the truth, and that the hearts of the wayward may return to the unity of Thy Church. Through our Lord. (Collect)

Thoughts

- Meekness is truly the character of Christianity because, through it, we submit to faith, to the promises of hope, and to the commandments of charity.

    —St. Robert, *FD*, p. 305

- Only God can make us happy by elevating and strengthening us.

    —St. Robert, *FD*, p. 219

Resolutions

1. Pray the Third Glorious Mystery, begging God to raise up in the Church holy bishops and cardinals.
2. Renew your retreat resolutions by trying to be more faithful to them.
3. Read a chapter of Christian doctrine for the purpose of handing on Catholic truth intelligently.

St. Pontius (of Cimiez)

May 14

God speaks to us

...she went down with him into the pit. And in bands she left him not, till she brought him the sceptre of the kingdom...
—Wisdom 10:13-14

Meditation

Two staunch pagans in Rome went up to the Temple of Jupiter. Senator Marcus and his wife Julia came to give thanks to the chief of the gods for a happy pregnancy that had just put an end to twenty-two years of sterility. They advanced towards the altar with their gifts, when a priest of Jupiter—with a menacing air—approached them, raving mad, and shouted at them: "Go back, accursed ones! How dare you enter this place carrying him who will become the enemy of our gods? Leave!" The couple did not understand his untimely intervention but left, seeking refuge in a nearby house. After reflection, Julia, not wishing to give birth to an enemy of the gods, was looking for how to kill her child. At his birth she dreamt of strangling him when her husband said: "Let Jupiter himself take revenge on his enemy." So it was that Pontius (d. 258) had his life spared. Although entrance into the Temple of Jupiter was forbidden to him, he went to school, where he attracted notice by the liveliness of his intellect and memory.

One morning while walking to the house of a professor, he heard in the street some voices chanting Psalm 113, where the psalmist says in speaking of the idols: "They have mouths and speak not, they have ears and hear not, they have feet and walk not..." While Pontius wondered what these words meant, at the end of the ceremony Pope Pontian (d. 235) told him the meaning. He told Pontius that the false gods, being only material creations, are absolutely powerless to help men. On the other hand, the true God, having a spiritual nature, is all-powerful, and He reveals Himself to those who seek Him. Pontius, touched by these comments, let the Pope know that his mother was dead, but that his father was still very attached to the worship of the gods. The Pope reassured him, explaining that God can convert him as He enlightened Pontius himself. In fact, shortly thereafter, his father joined as a catechumen and received Baptism with Pontius from the hands of the Pope.

After the death of his father, Pontius inherited his position and his fortune. As a senator, he gained the friendship of the emperors. However, Decius, upon his accession to power, issued an edict of persecution against Christians. Pontius hid himself in Rome; then he went to Cimiez, today in the Maritime Alps, near Nice. He was arrested there under Valerian (253-260) by the president Claudius, and after having been hung on the rack, exposed to beasts without feeling any pain, and placed on a pyre without being consumed by the flames, he finally had his head cut off with the stroke of an ax.

Prayer

O God, Who art the crown of Thy faithful, grant us the incessant patronage of blessed Pontius, Thy martyr, so that we might feel the effects of a continual intercession before Thee, of him whom the court of an earthly government had as a preacher. Through Jesus Christ. (Collect)

Thoughts

- By means of the cross, holy love perfects the loving soul, which offers it a fervent and generous heart.
 —St. Paul of the Cross, *PPJ*, June 1

- To carry one's cross means to carry not just any cross, but our own, the one that God gives us.
 —Charles de Foucauld, *PPJ*, October 15

Resolutions

1 Read Psalm 113, the fifth psalm of Sunday Vespers.

2 Pray for persecuted Christians and the martyrs of Islam.

3 Renounce idols: such and such a singer, such and such an actor, such and such an athlete...

St. John Baptist de la Salle

May 15

God speaks to us

Suffer the little children to come unto me...

—Mark 10:14

Meditation

John Baptist de la Salle (1651-1719) was born in Reims to parents who lived by their profound faith and solid virtues. From his earliest childhood, he showed great piety. When he cried, it was enough to show him a crucifix for him to be soothed. He loved to serve Mass and enjoyed reading the lives of the saints. At the death of his parents, being the oldest of seven children, the youngest of whom was only six years old, he acted as head of the family. Ordained a priest in 1678, he was promoted to canon of the Cathedral of Reims, then he began to deal with the education of the children of the common people, founding in 1684 the Institute of the Brothers of the Christian Schools. He carried out his mission for thirty-five years with tireless courage in the midst of the most complicated difficulties.

John's interior life was a constant striving for holiness. He accepted labor with joy and sufferings with love; he sought humiliations, sacrifices—in a word: the cross. He had only one love, Jesus Christ, and only one intention: to imitate Him. Wishing to make himself poor, the better to reach the poor whom he evangelized, he gave up his stately mansion so as to make it the first teacher training school, and then moved into a modest home. He gave to the poor the considerable fortune that he had inherited. In order to submit his body to his soul, he imposed austere mortifications on himself.

To that were added different exterior trials: he was the victim of jealousy, injustices, and persecutions; his family did not understand his attitude; some magistrates condemned him; priests afflicted him; several of his discouraged children abandoned him. In the midst of these difficulties, he did not lose courage, but kept his spirits up so as to meet all his obligations. In Reims, assisted by twelve teachers, he opened his institute, which very quickly became a flourishing one. He spread out in France, then in Europe, and soon to all five continents. One of the reasons for his success came from his happy initiatives which responded to the needs of his times. The students were grouped into distinct classes; order and discipline were required; the instruction was given in French and no longer in Latin, and was followed by suitable rewards and punishments. Since faith is the guardian of morals, religion was at the foundation of his teaching. Having completed his task, Saint John Baptist de la Salle finished his earthly pilgrimage on Good Friday, at the age of sixty-eight.

Patronage

Saint John Baptist de la Salle is the patron of educators.

Prayer

O God, Who didst raise up the holy Confessor John Baptist to promote the Christian education of the poor and to confirm the young in the way of truth, and through him didst beget a new family within Thy Church: mercifully grant, through his prayers and example, that we may burn with zeal for Thy glory in the salvation of souls, and become worthy to share in his heavenly crown. Through our Lord. (Collect)

Thoughts

- Make sure, by your zeal, to give tangible signs that you love those whom God has entrusted to you, as Jesus loved his Church.

  —St. John Baptist de la Salle

- I adore God's provisions for me in everything.

  —St. John Baptist de la Salle, his last words

Resolutions

1 Pray the Fourth Sorrowful Mystery for children in difficulty and for Catholic educators.
2 Send your children to staunchly Catholic schools.
3 Support good schools.

St. John Nepomucene

May 16

God speaks to us

If any man offend not in word, the same is a perfect man.
—James 3:2

Meditation

John Nepomucene (1330-1383) was born in Nepomuk (Bohemia), following the fervent prayers of his parents, who were still childless at an advanced age. Despite his weak constitution, he survived, so well that his mother hastened to consecrate him to Our Lord. Very soon, John manifested signs of great piety, serving several Masses each day. He undertook brilliant studies which resulted in his earning a doctorate of theology and of canon law. Once ordained a priest, he edified the faithful by his eloquence, which earned him promotion to canon of the Cathedral of Prague.

Wenceslas IV, succeeding his father as King of Bohemia in 1363, asked John to preach during Lent at the court. Moved by the sermons of the holy priest, Wenceslaus promised to struggle against laziness and debauchery, but these good resolutions did not last very long. John next became chaplain to the Queen Joanna. He encouraged her to keep calm, despite the mood swings of her fickle and violent husband. However, in time, the faults of the king became more pronounced. Much in love with his wife, he found himself prey to jealousy. After he became Emperor in 1378, Wenceslaus was still more imperious and suspicious. Intrigued by the length of his wife's confessions, he wanted to know what they contained. He asked the holy priest, who refused to violate the secrecy of confession. The following day, Wenceslaus was served an undercooked roast at the table. Immediately, he ordered that the chef be put on the spit. Saint John, indignant, threatened Wenceslaus with the wrath of God. The Emperor, furious at being contradicted, commanded that the priest be thrown in prison, and used the opportunity to try again to find out the content of the queen's confession. When the saint refused, he ordered him to be thrown over the city bridge into the Moldau River. His body was found and buried with great veneration.

Later, during John's exhumation in 1719, his body was seen stripped of its flesh, yet, miraculously, his tongue remained intact, the tongue that had refused to reveal the secret of confession.

Attributes, Invocation, and Patronage

Saint John Nepomucene is depicted as a canon with a surplice and a red biretta, contemplating a crucifix. He is invoked against floods, indiscretions, calumny, and for making a good confession. He is the patron of boatmen and the protector of bridges.

Prayer

O God, Whose Church the unconquerable sacramental silence of blessed John has enriched with yet another martyr's crown: grant that, strengthened by his prayers and example, we may set a guard upon our tongue, and be ready to endure any suffering the world can inflict, rather than risk the loss of our soul. Through our Lord. (Collect)

Thoughts

- Talking too much is harmful, says a proverb; on the other hand, when we do not talk too much, we usually can be glad about it.

   —Msgr. Chevrot, *VF*, p. 32

- Jesus crucified, Him alone, faithful friend between my frozen fingers, I will take to my grave.

   —St. Bernadette, *PPJ*, August 30

Resolutions

1 Pray the Third Glorious Mystery for the intention that our country will have leaders who promote the social doctrine of the Church.

2 Make a good examination of conscience in view of your next confession, notably on sins of the tongue.

3 Reduce idle chatter, texting, and e-mails.

St. Pascal Baylon

May 17

God speaks to us

He that eateth my flesh, and drinketh my blood, hath everlasting life.

—John 6:55

Meditation

Pascal Baylon (1540-1592) was born in the Kingdom of Aragon (Spain) to humble farmers. Very soon he was favored with ecstasies and showed a great devotion to the Blessed Virgin and to Jesus in the Blessed Sacrament. When he watched the flocks and heard the church bell sound at the consecration, he prostrated himself with a profound respect to adore the Divine Master. He showed also a tender compassion to the poor by giving them a few coins from his meager income. At the age of twenty-four, he entered the Franciscans as a lay brother. In the Order he was assigned the job of porter and cellarer, and sometimes that of collector, cook, or gardener. He would have liked to prolong his prayer time, but he was always faithful to the job that had been assigned to him. At table he chose for himself the portions that were less good. Moreover, he practiced frequent and severe bodily mortifications. Drawing his strength from Holy Communion, he gave himself only three hours of sleep a night. He spent hours before the tabernacle, often rapt in God, sometimes even levitating.

To his neighbor he showed the greatest charity. He was affable, cheerful, discreet, and faithful. He always found just the right words to console the afflicted; he worked healings and brought many sinners to repentance.

Becoming ill, he received eight days later the last rites and rendered his soul to God on Pentecost Sunday, at the precise moment of the elevation of the Sacred Host. During his funeral Mass, his eyes opened again at the moment of the two elevations of the host and the chalice. The miracle was recognized by Holy Church. Since his death, a strange phenomenon has happened many times at his tomb. When the saint wanted to herald public misfortunes or give a severe warning, resounding knocks were heard in front of his shrine.

Saint Pascal, pray to Jesus to give me a great love for the Eucharist, and do not let me approach this sacrament without having gone to confession first, if unfortunately I fall one day into a serious sin.

Attributes and patronage

Saint Pascal's attributes are a chalice surmounted by a host. He is the patron saint of congresses and Eucharistic works.

Prayer

O sweetest bread, heal the palate of my heart so that it may taste the sweetness of your love; heal it of all evil, so that it tastes no other sweetness than yours.

—Prayer of Saint Pascal before Communion

Or:

Truly divine bread, tear me from myself, receive me into you, for in you I live and in you I die.'

—Song of Saint Pascal

Thoughts

- Let us all go, let us approach the place where there are true grandeurs, for God is under [the appearances of] this bread.

    —St. Pascal

- We should have for God the heart of a child; for our neighbor, the heart of a mother; for oneself, the heart of a judge.

    —Maxim of Saint Pascal

Resolutions

1 Make a spiritual communion. (See Appendix.)

2 Adore the Blessed Sacrament in silence for fifteen minutes.

3 Unite yourself spiritually with the Masses celebrated during the day by repeating: "My God, I believe, I adore, I hope, and I love You. I ask You to pardon all those who do not believe, who do not adore, who do not hope, and who do not love You."

St. Felix of Cantalice

May 18

God speaks to us

And let the peace of Christ rejoice in your hearts, wherein also you are called in one body: and be ye thankful.
—Colossians 3:15

Meditation

Felix of Cantalice (1513-1587) was born at the foot of the Apennines (Italy), into a family of modest farmers. Charged with guarding the flocks, he carved a cross on an oak tree and, while his companions napped, he meditated for a long time on his knees in front of it. At thirty years of age, he decided to enter the Capuchins, a particularly austere religious Order. He explained his motivations to a friend: "I want," he said, 'to be religious for good, or not commit." The rising at night, the disciplines, the fasting, and the bare feet, did not weaken his determination. One day, upon entering the library of a benefactor, he exclaimed before a crucifix: "There is the book giving the key to all the others!" It is in this book that he would glean the knowledge and the secret of perseverance.

For forty years, he would serve as collector. To carry out his mission in the streets of Rome, he set himself the objective of maintaining "eyes on the ground, hand on the rosary, and heart in heaven." His language always reflected honesty, simplicity, and faith. A grateful soul, he tirelessly repeated in every circumstance of his life: *Deo gratias (Thanks be to God)!* Humble soul, he considered himself the vilest of creatures, calling out one day to the crowd pressing on him from all sides: "Let the Capuchin donkey pass."

An apostolic soul, he offered himself as an expiating victim. One night, a confrere heard him exclaim: "Lord, I recommend these poor people…Have mercy, great God! Have mercy on them!" To win souls to Jesus Christ, he multiplied rigorous fasting, he used bloody disciplines, and he slept no more than two or three hours per night on a plank.

The good Lord favored him with the gift of bilocation. Even before he entered the convent, while he was attending Mass, he was seen at the same time in the meadow tending the sheep. He was such a friend of God that one day he received the favor of holding the holy Infant Jesus and pressing Him to his heart.

Two years before his death, when the plague broke out in Rome, he hastened to help the sick. He healed many by a simple sign of the cross. At last he died, visited by an apparition of the Blessed Virgin, who came looking for him to lead him to paradise.

INVOCATION

Saint Felix is invoked to have a powerful voice.

PRAYER

[Most Blessed Virgin Mary], august Virgin, I desire to love you as a good son; and, like a good mother, do not take your helping hand from me, for I am like those little children who cannot take a single step of their own accord, and who fall if the support of their mother fails them.

—St. Felix, *Au. S.,* II, p. 226

THOUGHTS

- Of science, I do not know anything but the Holy Cross.
—St. Felix, *Au. S.,* II, p. 226

- I would like to know only six letters, five red and one white: the five red letters are the five wounds of the Savior, and the white letter is His most holy Mother.
—St. Felix, *Au. S.,* II, p. 226

RESOLUTIONS

1 Pray the Fourth Glorious Mystery, asking the Blessed Virgin for the grace of perseverance, and in praying for the dying.

2 Remove useless books from your library.

3 In the streets, practice modesty of the eyes.

St. Yves

May 19

God speaks to us

In judging be merciful to the fatherless as a father, and as a husband to their mother. And thou shalt be as the obedient son of the Most High; and He will have mercy on thee more than a mother.

—Ecclesiasticus 4:10-11

Meditation

Yves (1253-1303) was born in Kermartin (Côtes-d'Armor, Brittany) to a very pious mother who gave him the love of God and of the saints. He had but one desire: also to become a saint. From his youngest years, he acquired a great devotion to Our Lady, reciting daily the Little Office of the Blessed Virgin. Once a student, he followed the course of theology, of civil and canon law in Paris and then in Orléans. He was already a model of purity and penance.

At the age of twenty-seven, Yves was appointed an ecclesiastical judge by the Bishop of Rennes; then some years later he was transferred to his Diocese (Tréguier) where he received the priesthood. As a judge, he considered himself above all as the protector of the poor, the widow and, the orphan, and as the defender of the weak, even going so far as to take charge of all the expenses that they were obliged to pay. To defend them only one thing mattered: their rights, and he knew how to assert them, even against important people and his own friends. He was not a respecter of persons, remembering that he was only the instrument of the Supreme Judge who one day will reward everyone according to his works. Only bad faith made him inflexible.

In 1288, Yves was named pastor of the parish in Trédez, and four years later, of the parish in Louannec, near Perros-Guirec (Côtes-d'Armor). On his arrival in Louannec his parishioners were hardly devout, but before long they were won over by his gentleness, modesty, and self-denial. In order to convert his parish he relied above all on prayer and penance. The sick were the object of his most tender care. He invited them to unite their sufferings to those of the Divine Master. The poor experienced in their turn the blessings of his charity. One day, he took in a leper whom he cared for kindly when, in the middle of his meal, he said to him: "The Lord is with you," then his face became resplendent; the saint recognized Jesus. Four days before his death, he celebrated Mass for the last time, and at dawn on May 19 he went to meet his Divine Savior.

Attributes and patronage

Dressed in the robes of a lawyer and often wearing a red biretta, Saint Yves holds in his hand the text of a lawsuit. In Brittany he was surrounded by rich and poor. He is the patron of lawyers, notaries, bailiffs, and orphans, and of Brittany.

Prayer

O God, who hast chosen Thy illustrious confessor blessed Yves as minister for the salvation of souls and the defense of the poor, grant us grace to imitate his charity and to be protected by his patronage with Thee. By Our Lord. (Collect)

Thoughts

- You must fill yourself with the spirit of Our Lord, so that it can be seen that you love Him and that you seek to make Him loved.
    —St. Vincent de Paul, *PPJ*, October 25

- We cannot better ensure our eternal happiness than by living and dying as servants of the poor.
    —St. Vincent de Paul, *PPJ*, September 29

Resolutions

1 Pray the Fourth Sorrowful Mystery for a family affected by the death of a father or a mother.

2 Defend the weak when they are treated unjustly.

3 Make a donation to a poor person or to a good work.

St. Bernardine of Siena

May 20

God speaks to us

That in the name of Jesus every knee should bow, of those that are in heaven, on earth, and under the earth:
—Philippians 2:10

Meditation

Bernardine of Siena (1380-1444) came into the world in the year of the death of Saint Catherine to continue the work of the humble Dominican. As a child, he blushed at the slightest inappropriate word, as if he had been slapped. Bernardine derived his virtue of purity from his love towards the Blessed Virgin. During a plague epidemic, he braved death a hundred times to treat and bury the plague victims. At twenty years of age, Bernardine entered the Franciscans and soon stirred up crowds by his preaching. Those were conducted in the open air on account of the great number of listeners. While Bernardine only had a hoarse, ugly voice, the Blessed Virgin gave him in due time a harmonious and dazzling voice, capable of captivating crowds and touching hearts.

What attracted people to Bernardine were his terrifying words against sin, but with a singular sweetness towards the sinner. His face beamed with joy; he lived in peace and spread it around him. The world in that era was divided by political quarrels. We can already see the rebellious heresies of Wycliffe and John Huss emerging.

In Bologna he spoke against gamblers. In Florence, he stigmatized the use of jewels and other objects of women's vanity; in these two cities, he built a pyre in which he burnt games, wigs, cosmetics, and mirrors as the crowd applauded. In Perugia, a city known for its moral decline, to attract the inhabitants, he announced to them that he was going to show them the devil. Once assembled around him, they heard him say: "This is not one devil I am going to show you, but several. Are you not devils, you who do the works of Satan?" He then enumerated their vices and managed to touch their hearts so that they were reconciled with God. In addition, Saint Bernardine revived the devotion to the holy name of Jesus by having engraved on the public and private monuments the trigrammaton "IHS" which means "Jesus Savior of Men." At the end of each of his sermons he had someone engrave a memorial plaque with the three letters. Thanks to him, the devotion to the Holy Name of Jesus would spread through the whole Church. Bernardine died content, his task accomplished, like a good worker.

Attributes

Saint Bernardine of Siena's attribute is a disc on which is inscribed the trigrammaton IHS, surrounded by flames. Three miters are sometimes attached to his feet in allusion to the three bishoprics of Siena, Ferrara, and Urbino, which he declined.

Prayer

O Lord Jesus Christ, Who didst grant to blessed Bernardine, Thy Confessor, a surpassing love for Thy Holy Name: we beseech Thee, by his merits and intercession, graciously pour into our hearts the spirit of Thy love: Who livest and reignest. (Collect)

Thoughts

- Just as you worship Jesus in his flesh, so also you must worship the name of Jesus.

—St. Bernardine

- All the heavenly gifts, all the virtues, and all the graces are dispensed by the hands of Mary and she shares them with whom she wants, when she wants.

—St. Bernardine. *Sermon 5 on the Nativity,* ch. 8

Resolutions

1 Invoke the Name of Jesus above all in sorrows, difficulties, and temptations.

2 Listen to sermons with more attention and draw some lessons for your daily life.

3 Get rid of an object that feeds your vanity.

St. Gisela, Abbess of Chelles

May 21

God speaks to us

Favour is deceitful, and beauty is vain: the woman that feareth the Lord, she shall be praised.

—Proverbs 31:30

Meditation

Gisela or Isbergue (753-807) was the daughter of Pepin the Short and Queen Bertha, and thus the sister of Charlemagne. She was blessed to have for her godfather Pope Stephen II (d. 757). The tie established between the Pope and the King of the Franks by her Baptism encouraged Pepin to come to the aid of the Supreme Pontiff in his struggle against the Lombards. As for Gisela, she grew up at the castle of Aire-sur-la-Lys (Nord-Pas-de-Calais). Her older brother, Charlemagne, greatly appreciated her for her beauty, and above all for her virtue. To avoid a fall into worldliness, Gisela took for her spiritual director Venant, perhaps a relative of hers, who had just retired not far from the castle where she lived in order to lead a life of ardent prayer. Following a battle during which he had been seriously wounded in the leg, Venant definitively abandoned the vanities of the world. From then on, he sought only God. We have no account of the conversation between these two young people, but we know that at the end, Gisela promised before God to preserve holy virginity.

However, a little after, a prince of the land of Wales or of Scotland, hearing of her distinguished qualities and great beauty, desired to marry her. Gisela's parents pressed her to accept him. She asked for one night to reflect and pray to the good Lord to take away her physical beauty. Her wish was granted. She found herself at that very moment afflicted with a hideous leprosy which made her repulsive. The suitor, seized with horror upon seeing her, quickly returned home. A little later, Gisela regained her health.

After the death of Pepin, Bertha took over the governance of the kingdom. The Lombards, with their King Didier, continued to be a menace to the Pope and to France. And so, Bertha thought of marrying her three children to those of Didier. Gisela obstinately refused, despite the insistence of her mother, who explained to her that the welfare of the kingdom was at stake. Happily, the Pope supported her in her refusal. A little after, Gisela embraced the Benedictine life at Aire, training there other young girls by her example. She lived the last thirty years of her life there and was buried near Saint Venant, who, a little before she had entered the convent, had received the martyr's palm.

Invocation

Saint Gisela is invoked to obtain the healing of fever, complaints of the skin, and deformities.

Prayer

O God, who rescued blessed Gisela from the contagion of the century to lead her to Christ, grant us, following her example and through her intercession, to be neither corrupted by malice nor deceived by the lies of the world.' Through Jesus Christ. (Collect)

Thoughts

- This leper, it is you, if you are in a state of mortal sin. By the sin, you are condemned to death, to eternal death, to hell.

    —St. Alphonsus de Liguori, *SJJ*, p. 198

- To reward our deeds, God will value them by the weight of the purity of intention that we have had in doing them.

    —St. Mary Magdalene de' Pazzi

Resolutions

1. Work at putting yourself in the presence of God in order to improve the quality of your prayers.
2. Avoid flirtatiousness, remembering that our mortal body, an object of concupiscence, is destined to rot in the earth.
3. Fulfill the duty of your state in life instead of satisfying your little desires, and thus do God's will always.

St. Rita

May 22

God speaks to us

In your patience you shall possess your souls.
—Luke 21:19

Meditation

Saint Margaret, nicknamed Rita (1381-1457), was born in Umbria in the town of Cascia (Italy). When she was twelve years old, she manifested a desire to serve God in the religious life, but her parents, already far advanced in age, judged it more prudent for her to marry. Rita submitted humbly. However, the choice of suitor was most unfortunate. Very quickly after the marriage he proved to be violent. Their eighteen years of common life were for her a true Calvary. Despite everything, though, by her sweetness and patience, Rita finally converted her husband, who died under the blows of his enemies a short time later. Once again, Rita accepted the mysterious designs of Providence and forgave the murderers. A little later, she endured the trial of the death of her two sons.

Freed from all obligations in the world, Rita wished to fulfill her youthful dream by entering the Augustinian nuns of Cascia, but she found herself rejected by the superior because their community, on principle, admitted virgins only. Rita was not discouraged, however. She prayed with all her heart to three of her favorite saints: Saint John the Baptist, Saint Augustine, and Saint Nicolas of Tolentine, who soon appeared to her. They brought her into the monastery, whose doors were all closed. Immediately the superior accepted her, with enthusiasm.

The saint led there an extremely mortified life, wearing a hair shirt, and fasting often on bread and water. After a sermon on the Passion, she asked Our Lord for the grace to participate in His sufferings. She then felt the pain of the crown of thorns, and her forehead was marked for life by a painful wound which gave off a bad odor, obliging her into forced retirement deep in the convent. Her patience in this trial was heroic. The good Lord rewarded her by granting her the gift of miracles. A four-year-long illness completed the purification. Sensing her imminent death, she received Extreme Unction at her request, then she exhorted the nuns to observe the rule correctly, before falling asleep in the Lord.

Invocation and patronage

Saint Rita is invoked against smallpox as well as in difficult and desperate cases. She is the patroness of pork butchers.

Prayer

O God, Thou didst confer on Saint Rita the great graces of loving her enemies and of bearing on her brow the marks of Thy love and Thy passion. Through her prayers and merits may we forgive our enemies and dwell upon the sufferings of Thy passion and so receive the rewards promised to the humble and to those who mourn: Who livest and reignest. (Collect)

Thoughts

- Not only must we be careful to keep harshness and impatience away from ourselves, but we must also strive to serve others with cordiality and great gentleness, even the most annoying and difficult.

  —St. Vincent de Paul, *R*, p. 9

- When Judgment Day comes, how happy we will be about our misfortunes, proud of our humiliations, and rich by our sacrifices!

  —St. John Vianney, *PPJ*, November 17

Resolutions

1 Pray a *Memorare* (see Appendix) for a husband or a wife whose husband is particularly hard to get along with and add three invocations to Saint Rita.

2 Suffer without complaining and be in a good mood when others care for you.

3 Offer up in advance the annoyances of the day.

St. Didier

May 23

GOD SPEAKS TO US

The Good Shepherd giveth His life for His sheep.
—Saint John 10:11

MEDITATION

Today the Church celebrates two saints by the same name. Both were bishops and martyrs. The first was Bishop of Langres (d. around 407), the second—Bishop of Vienne (d. 606-607); the first was born in Genoa, received no instruction, lived in Champagne and died in Langres; the second was born in Bourgogne, was a man of letters, ministered zealously in the ancient province of Dauphiné and died in Les Dombes, in the village that took the name Saint-Didier-sur-Chalaronne.

Saint Didier of Langres, who is the object of our meditation, was born in the countryside to a poor family, and he liked to converse with God in that very simple, laborious life. Very early on, his soul was adorned with the virtues belonging to his state. Since Langres was without a bishop at that time, God made it known that the one He destined to ascend to that see was someone named Didier. Several men were sent on the providential mission to go find him, and were to recognize him by a second sign: at his approach, the staff that he will hold in his hand will be covered with leaves and flowers. They traveled therefore to the vicinity of Genoa (Italy) and recognized him when he gave his name, and they saw at that same moment his staff flowering. Didier at first refused their offer, but convinced by the providential signs, he finally accepted.

His apostolate was guided from start to finish by Divine Providence. Docile to grace, he did extraordinary good by the brilliance of his teaching and his good sense in governing. He excelled by the firmness of his faith and the extent of his charity in the midst of many contradictions, which won for him the respect and love of his people.

St. Didier

As Christianity developed in his diocese, all that he lacked now was the grace of martyrdom. It was granted to him by the Vandals, those barbarians who already had extended their ravages in Southern France and in the region around Lyons. When the city of Langres was besieged, Didier went to visit the enemy chief to pacify him and to become the advocate of his people, but the latter had him arrested. The holy bishop offered his life for the safety of his faithful and then was decapitated outside the walls of the city.

Saint Didier, ask Jesus to help me to stay firm in the faith and to be docile to the inspirations of the Holy Ghost, so that I may extend His kingdom around me.

Attribute and patronage

Saint Didier is depicted decapitated with his head in his hands. He is the patron of the cities of Langres, Saint-Dizier, Avignon, Arles, Genoa, and Bologna.

Prayer

Grant, Lord, we beseech Thee, that the prayers of Saint Didier, Bishop and Martyr, may come to our aid, so that what we cannot obtain by ourselves, Thou wouldst deign to bestow on us through his powerful intercession, through Jesus Christ our Lord.

—Prayer, *PS* II, p. 92

Thoughts

- God asks for courageous souls and loves them, provided that they are humble and do not trust in themselves at all.

  —St. Teresa of Avila, *PPJ*, October 25

- Strike the shepherd, but spare the flock!

  —Hymn for First Vespers of St. Didier

Resolutions

1 Recite the Fifth Glorious Mystery, asking God to raise up a new Saint Didier to convert our contemporaries.

2 Recite an Act of Faith from the depth of your hear. (See Appendix.)

3 Set a little rule for your life, a program for your days. Submit it to your spiritual guide, and be faithful to it.

St. Vincent of Lerins

May 24

God speaks to us

Keep that which is committed to thy trust, avoiding the profane novelties of words.
—First Epistle of Saint Paul to Timothy, 6:20

Meditation

Saint Vincent of Lerins (d. 450) was the brother of Saint Lupus of Troyes. He was born, no doubt, in the vicinity of Toul, and it is thought that he at first enlisted in the army. He himself explains his decision to leave the world: "Tossed about by the various sad whirlwinds of the era, I finally hid myself in the port of religion, that sweet refuge of man. There, putting aside all thoughts of pride and vanity, appeasing God by the sacrifice of Christian humility, I seek to avoid not only the shipwrecks of the present life, but also the eternal flames." Saint Vincent was aware that life on earth is an immense blessing that must not be squandered, for the day will come when the good Lord will ask us how we led our life. In order to make his as fruitful as possible, he decided to withdraw to Lerins, the island where Saint Honoratus had founded several schools some time earlier. Some young noblemen came there to study the humanities, but Vincent wished above all to acquire divine knowledge there.

Whereas three years earlier the Church had just condemned Nestorius, who claimed that the Blessed Virgin is not the Mother of God, Vincent composed his *Commonitorium*, in other words, his *Rule of Conduct*, truly a golden book, rich in arguments explaining the signs of membership in the true Church founded by Jesus Christ. He shone by his humility: he did not even sign his work. At the beginning of his work, he poses the question: "How can Catholic truth be distinguished from error and heresies?" And he answers: "We know Catholic truth by the divine authority of the Scriptures, and by the Tradition of the Catholic Church." Tradition is the oral transmission of the truths of the faith. It gives the correct interpretation of the Scriptural texts, since they are not understood in the same way by everyone. Saint Vincent clarifies: "In the Catholic Church itself, it is necessary to take great care to hold fast to what has been believed everywhere, always, and by everyone." But then, some will say, "If the criterion of catholicity is antiquity, is development not possible?" The holy theologian replies: "Although there is novelty in your style, let there be none in your teaching. Let there be progress, not change."

As a child becomes an adult, then an old man, while remaining the same human being, so too dogma flourishes, but while preserving the same substance, the same meaning, the same idea.

In an era when many Catholics allow themselves to be attracted by the love of novelties, help us, Saint Vincent, to preserve the faith of our ancestors so as to attain one day the blessed eternity of Heaven.

Prayer

O God, who dost gladden us by the yearly solemnity of Blessed Vincent, Thy Confessor, mercifully grant that, while celebrating his birth in heaven, we might also imitate the example of his life. Through Jesus Christ. (Collect)

Thoughts

- If time carries all things away, we too must snatch from it a few moments that will be profitable for us unto eternal life.

    —St. Vincent, *Commonitorium*

- God forbid that the rosebushes of Catholic dogma should turn into thistles and thorn bushes!

    —St. Vincent, *Commonitorium*

Resolutions

1. Recite the Creed with attention and devotion.
2. Take fifteen minutes during the day to unite yourself with God in a heart-to-heart conversation or to see how you can be pleasing to Him.
3. Read a chapter from the catechism or a book on doctrine.

St. Gregory VII
May 25

GOD SPEAKS TO US

Thou hast loved justice, and hated iniquity: therefore God, thy God, hath anointed thee with the oil of gladness.

—Psalm 44:8

MEDITATION

Hildebrand, the future Gregory VII (1015-1085), was the son of humble parents from Tuscany (Italy). He pursued his studies in Rome in a monastery where the abbot was his uncle. When he himself was appointed abbot of the monastery of Saint Paul Outside the Walls, he reformed it so well that the Pope sent him to France as a legate to fight against trafficking in ecclesiastical dignities (simony) and against the immoral life of the clergy. Hildebrand led the Bishop of Lyons to acknowledge that he had been elected because of simony, and, at the Council of Tours, he compelled Bérenger to renounce his heresy concerning the Eucharist and to acknowledge the real presence of Jesus in the Host after the consecration.

Upon being elected Pope in 1073, Gregory VII worked with such great zeal to strengthen ecclesiastical discipline, to spread the faith, to restore freedom to the Church, and to attack errors and vices that no pontiff since the time of the Apostles had undertaken as many labors as he.

He issued very rapidly the following norms: "He who has obtained sacred orders or an ecclesiastical dignity in exchange for money becomes by that very fact unfit to carry out a responsibility in the Church. Clerics who live with a concubine are forbidden to exercise any function whatsoever at the altar; if some contravene these regulations, the faithful may in no case attend their ceremonies." Soon sanctions followed the threats. Gregory VII deposed in particular the Bishops of Bremen and Bamberg, and suspended those of Strasbourg and Speyer. Since Henry IV, Emperor of Germany, had adopted the custom of conferring investiture on bishops and abbots, Saint Gregory put an end to this abuse of the civil authority with regard to the ecclesiastical authority. Furious at this decree, Henry IV induced twenty-four bishops to sign a declaration in Worms, in which they refused henceforth to recognize Gregory VII as Pope. He then excommunicated Henry IV and relieved his subjects of their oath of loyalty toward him. The Emperor found himself compelled to make amends honorably. He traveled barefoot to the residence of Countess Matilda of Tuscany, where the Pope had taken refuge, so as to submit to him. But soon Henry IV obliged Gregory VII, who had been Pontiff for twelve years, to leave Rome.

The Pope then traveled to Salerno, and from there he predicted the triumph of the Church. He died saying: "I loved justice and I hated iniquity; this is why I die in exile."

Prayer

O God, the strength of all those who put their trust in Thee, Thou didst fortify Blessed Gregory, Thy Confessor and Pontiff, with the virtue of constancy for the defense of the liberty of Thy Church; grant us by his example and intercession to overcome bravely all adversities. Through our Lord…

—Collect

Thoughts

- Without chastity, the other virtues are worthless, just as chastity loses its value unless it is accompanied by the other virtues.
  —St. Gregory VII, *Register of Letters*, II, 25.

- Since [I have been Pope], I have not stopped fighting to restore to this chaste Church of Christ her freedom, her splendor, and the purity of her ancient discipline.
  —St. Gregory VII

RESOLUTIONS

1 Pray to Saint Gregory VII to enlighten and support the Pope, so that he may proclaim the truth loud and clear to the world and that he may fight courageously against the current errors.

2 Be faithful to your commitments. Reflect on this from time to time in God's light.

3 Make sure to strengthen your faith by a pure life of integrity.

St. Philip Neri

May 26

God speaks to us

My heart grew hot within me: and in my meditation a fire shall flame out.

—Psalm 38:4

Meditation

Philip Neri (1515-1585) was born in Florence (Italy) of a mother who died shortly afterward and a father who was a notary. He was raised by the Dominican friars, to whom he would show the utmost gratitude throughout his life. In his late adolescence he arrived in Rome and would never leave it again. He already showed signs of great piety. In 1544, in the catacombs of Saint Sebastian, he had such an intense mystical experience that it caused him to have an expansion of the chest, resulting in two broken ribs. Only after a formal command did he agree to be ordained a priest at the age of thirty-six. During the celebration of the Holy Sacrifice of the Mass, he was so absorbed by the divine mysteries that he regularly started to levitate. He had to resort to various subterfuges to try not to be raised above the ground.

A humble man, he never stopped saying: "Lord, beware of Philip!" In his contacts with his neighbor, he strove to be everything to everyone. One day, upon meeting three Jews, he sought in vain to convert them. And so he hastened to say Mass for their intention. After the Holy Sacrifice was celebrated, the three men asked to be baptized. Philip also performed physical miracles. Cardinal Baronius benefited twice from his healing charism. As for Paul Fabricius, he died without a priest. Upon arriving at his remains, Philip revived him, heard his confession, and then Paul chose to die rather than to fall back into sin, and he died again, this time with his soul at peace. Philip was endowed with the gift of tears, and he wept so much that his contemporaries wondered how he could preserve his sight.

This did not prevent him from having a cheerful, very

shrewd, joyful personality. With these natural virtues he combined an acute understanding of human beings, which attracted many souls to him, especially young people. He loved to meet them as they left their school or their workshop so as to converse with them and to guide them spiritually. In 1575 he founded the Congregation of the Oratory with fourteen companions. He agreed to be the superior only when the Pope ordered it. The Holy Father entrusted to him the Church of Santa Maria in Vallicella, in the very heart of Rome. For the last twenty years of his life, he assumed the responsibility of serving as spiritual director to cardinals, men of the Curia and of the royal court, and even to popes, noblemen, and the common people, so that he became the most popular personage of the second half of the 16th century. Saint Ignatius of Loyola held him in very high esteem. At his death, all Rome mourned him.

Prayer

O God, Thou didst raise up Blessed Philip, Thy Confessor, to the glory of Thy Saints; mercifully grant, that we who rejoice in his feast may profit by the example of his virtues. Through our Lord… (Collect)

Thoughts

- Let everyone strive for purity of heart, for the Holy Ghost dwells in simple, candid souls.

  —St. Philip

- We must accept the trials that God sends us without superfluous discussion, and consider it certain that this course of action is what is best for us.

  —St. Philip

Resolutions

1 Recite the First Sorrowful Mystery, imploring the conversion of a sinner.

2 Make an effort to act always with a pure intention so as to draw down God's blessings.

3 Take the time to listen to young people and to guide them.

St. Bede the Venerable

May 27

GOD SPEAKS TO US

The mouth of the just shall meditate wisdom, and his tongue shall speak judgment.

—Psalm 36:30

MEDITATION

Born in Great Britain, Bede (673-735) was an orphan from the age of seven. He was entrusted to Saint Biscop, then to Saint Ceolfrith, Benedictine abbots, then consecrated his life to God in the shadow of the cloister in Jarrow (England). He was ordained a deacon at the age of eighteen and a priest at the age of thirty.

Since he liked very much to learn, to teach, and to write, he divided his life between prayer, manual labor, and study according to the famous formula that is so dear to the Benedictines: *"Ora et labora*, Pray and work."

His knowledge was very extensive: Latin, Greek, poetry, the exact sciences, Sacred Scripture, and Church history enriched his mind, but he was brilliant especially in the last two disciplines, to the point of meriting the glorious title of "Doctor of the Church."

In his commentaries on Sacred Scripture, he gave preference to the allegorical sense over the literal sense, and he relied much on the Fathers of the Church, adding to them a personal touch. He had a clear, simple mind, pure doctrine, imbued by the spirit of faith, modesty, and piety. He perfectly united knowledge and faith, with both of them strengthening his soul in goodness.

This union was evident until the end of his life. Indeed, the monk Cuthbert, his disciple, related his last moments in this earthly exile as follows. Bede, despite his great physical weakness, pursued his usual activities, going from prayer to study and from study to prayer. On the day of his death, he was correcting an English translation of Saint Isidore of Seville, when his disciple pointed out to him that he seemed very tired and it would be better for him to stop. Only one chapter was left to correct. Bede then told him to take the pen and to write as fast as he could. Then, as soon as the work was finished, the disciple told him, "It is finished." And Bede replied: "You are right, it is indeed finished." A great lover of the Divine Office, he then prostrated himself while reciting the words: *Gloria Patri, et Filio, et Spiritui Sancto*, and expired.

The custom of calling him "the Venerable" spread in the ninth century. Already during his lifetime he had considerable influence, but throughout the Middle Ages he was, after Saints Augustine, Jerome, Ambrose, Gregory the Great, and Isidore, one of the authors most often read.

Prayer

O God, Thou dost glorify Thy Church by the learning of Blessed Bede, Thy Confessor and Doctor; mercifully grant to Thy servants always to be enlightened by his wisdom, and helped by his merits. Through our Lord...
(Collect)

Thoughts

- The Mother of God is blessed to have contributed to the Incarnation of the Word, but she is even more blessed to have merited, by loving Him always, to keep Him in her eternally.

    —St. Bede, Book IV, chap. 49 on St. Luke

- The only way to show that Christ dwells in you is the spirit of holy and undivided charity, so that, having become one body of Christ through communion, you may not be separated from the unity of this body through the spirit of dissension.

    —St. Bede, *PL*, 90, 51-52.

Resolutions

1 Recite the First Joyful Mystery to thank the Blessed Virgin for having agreed to become the Mother of God.

2 Read a chapter of the New Testament or the Gospel of the day in your missal.

3 Show a great spirit of charity, especially in your family.

St. Germain of Paris

May 28

GOD SPEAKS TO US

There was not found the like of him in glory, who kept the law of the Most High and was in covenant with Him. Therefore by an oath He gave him glory in his posterity, that he should increase.

—Ecclesiasticus 44:20, 22

MEDITATION

Germain or Germanus (496-576) was born in Autun of an unnatural mother, and his grandmother showed him no more affection during his studies in Avallon. Fortunately, he received a much warmer welcome in the home of his uncle in Luzy (Nièvre). There he learned both the fear of God and knowledge of Scripture. At the age of fifteen, having already displayed a high degree of virtue, he was ordained a deacon, and three years later he was raised to the priestly dignity. Continuing to grow in holiness, he was soon appointed abbot of the Monastery of Saint Symphorien in Autun, where he gave good example of a life of prayer and penance. Around the year 555, the Bishop of Paris, Eusebius, died, and Childebert I, King of the Franks, took advantage of the presence of Saint Germain in his city to designate him as the successor. The episcopal dignity did not lead the former monk to diminish the austerity of his life. He continued to observe the vigils and monastic fasts and to do without heat in the winter. But while seeking his own perfection, he did not neglect to care for his faithful and to show great generosity to the poor.

God blessed him by bestowing on him the gift of miracles. From the first years of his episcopate, Childebert was healed miraculously by him, which partly explains the great influence that Germain would later have with the King. Both men contributed to the foundation of the famous abbey which, after the saint's death, would take the name of Saint-Germain-des-Prés. The saint from Bourgogne sent for monks from Autun to fill the new monastery. After the death of Childebert, he maintained very good relations with Clotaire, his successor, and with the king's wife, Saint Radegonde. However, when Clotaire (d. 561) died in turn, Saint Germain tried in vain to mediate in the quarrels between Brunehaut against Frédégonde, the respective wives of two of Clotaire's four sons. He died at the age of eighty, loaded with merits.

Invocation

Saint Germain is invoked in childhood illnesses, particularly for infants who are slow in learning to walk, and also to obtain the early release of a person in prison.

Prayer

O Lord, who didst inspire Saint Germain with great zeal for Thy glory and such great charity for the unfortunate, grant us, we pray, through his merits and intercession, the grace to avoid all that may displease Thee, and to do faithfully what is pleasing to Thee, so that we might find therein the fulfillment of all our duties and the blessing of a good death. Through our Lord Jesus Christ…

—Prayer, *PS* II, p. 142.

Thoughts

- Through morning prayer you open the windows of your soul to the Sun of justice; through evening prayer you close them to the darkness of hell.

  —St. Francis de Sales, *PPJ*, May 16

- Make use of everyday annoyances to mortify yourself, accepting them lovingly and sweetly.

  —St. Francis de Sales, XXI, p. 168

Resolutions

1 Carefully say your evening prayers, and do not omit your examination of conscience.

2 Avoid quarrels in the family, especially between spouses; forgive one another and receive Holy Communion together.

3 Be a model in your professional work or your studies.

St. Mary Magdalene de Pazzi

May 29

GOD SPEAKS TO US

God forbid that I should glory, save in the cross of our Lord Jesus Christ.

—Saint Paul to the Galatians 6:14

MEDITATION

In the sixteenth century the Church was afflicted by the widespread ravages of Protestantism, but she was consoled by a magnificent constellation of saints, encouraging souls of good will to stay on their course to Heaven. At that time Catherine de Pazzi (1566-1607) was born in Florence (Italy). From the age of seven or eight she used to recite a prayer to the Holy Ghost and the *Confiteor*, and she abandoned herself to the love of God, which absorbed her to the point that she no longer heard or felt anything. At her First Holy Communion she vowed her virginity to Jesus and was ready to make all the necessary sacrifices.

At the age of sixteen she entered the Carmel and received the habit the following year, taking the name of Mary Magdalene, one of her favorite saints. Her fervor, punctuality, and love for the Rule were so great that the mistress of novices saw her more as a mistress than a novice. She then had the experience of suffering, which would be her instructress and companion throughout her life. She also had ecstasies and raptures during which she entered into an intimate knowledge of God. When her prayers were not answered, she went so far as to rejoice, telling herself that it was better to do God's will rather than her own. She was blessed with particular revelations. And so, at the death of Saint Aloysius Gonzaga, she saw his soul ascending to Heaven in a dazzling light.

These extraordinary graces were purchased at the price of greater sufferings. For five years she was prey to the most horrible temptations to pride, sensuality, despair, and doubt. She found refuge with Our Lady and imposed various austerities on herself. Her community assigned to her the responsibilities of mistress of novices and sub-prioress. She encouraged her subordinates to mortify their senses. "Beware of relaxation," she told them. "To violate one of our holy rules is to offend the apple of God's eye!"

During the last year of her life, afflicted by very severe sufferings, she exclaimed, "To suffer, but not to die! Not to die so soon, so as not to stop suffering so soon!" She died at the age of forty-one, after encouraging the sisters of her community to love God alone and to be ready to suffer anything for love of Him.

Attributes

Saint Mary Magdalene is depicted as a Carmelite, with a lighted candle and a crown of thorns.

Prayer

O God, the lover of virginity, Thou didst adorn with heavenly gifts Blessed Mary Magdalene, a virgin inflamed with Thy love; grant that we may imitate her in purity and charity, whom we venerate with festive celebration. Through our Lord... (Collect)

Thoughts

- Have the same purity in all your words and in all your actions as if they were the last ones of your life.

  —St. Mary Magdalene

- Never give advice without first consulting Jesus Christ nailed to the cross.

  —St. Mary Magdalene

Resolutions

1 Recite an Act of Charity. (See Appendix.)

2 Do the will of God, starting with what costs you the most.

3 Have recourse to Jesus on the cross before making any important decision.

St. Joan of Arc

May 30

God speaks to us

Thou hast done manfully, and thy heart has been strengthened...The hand of the Lord hath strengthened thee, and therefore thou shalt be blessed for ever.

—Judith 15:11

Meditation

The heroic life of St. Joan of Arc (1412-1431) is explained by her love for God, by her sense of duty, but also by her love for the Church. During her trial, she told her judges: "I love the Church; I would like to support her with all my power and to die for the Christian faith." The reason why she loved the Church so much was because it is identified with Jesus. "It seems to me," Joan said, "that Our Lord and the Church are one." Hence her deep attachment to all that the Church teaches.

"I love the Church," she protested before her judges; "I would never want to uphold anything against her faith." "I am baptized," she explained. "I am a good Christian, and I will die a good Christian." Nonetheless, her enemies, in order to justify their murder, declared her an "apostate, heretic, schismatic." A notice posted opposite the pyre on which she was to die bore this inscription. At the sight of it, Joan became indignant and exclaimed, "No, I am not a heretic; no, I am not schismatic; I am a good Christian!" Six hundred years later we cannot help being moved when we hear this cry of St. Joan. This is the testimony of a martyr who protests her innocence in the presence of her executioners. She hopes to gather all peoples under the scepter of Christ the King.

Her love for the Church is reflected also in the great respect that she had for its laws. Thus while in prison in Rouen she observed quite strictly the fast prescribed by the Church although she was not yet twenty years old. She submitted to the authority of the Church whenever she could.

When she was a child, she heard heavenly voices and spoke to her parish priest about them. Then, when she was summoned to Poitiers by an ecclesiastical commission, she patiently answered the most delicate questions about her revelations. Finally, she found herself on a third occasion in the presence of the Church's authorities, but this time for an unjust trial. Knowing that the men of the Church are not the Church, she exclaimed to the tribunal that was convened irregularly in order to condemn her, "I appeal to the Universal Church."

Unfortunately, her request was not granted; however the day would come when her case would be reexamined and she would be rehabilitated, by the voice of Pope Pius II (1458-1464), who was the first to speak highly of her.

O Saint Joan of Arc, pray to God that He may give me such great love for the Church that I may strive to honor it by my words and by a life that is in keeping with my dignity as a Christian.

Prayer

O God, who didst miraculously raise up the blessed virgin Joan to protect the faith and her fatherland, grant us, through her intercession, to see the Church triumph over the snares of her enemies and to enjoy perpetual peace. Through Jesus Christ our Lord. (Collect)

Thoughts

- "The Lord God is the first to be served!"

    —St. Joan of Arc

- "The men of arms will battle, and God will give the victory.'

    —St. Joan of Arc

Resolutions

1 Carefully say your morning prayers so as to give God first place in your day.
2 Obey the Church by observing the precepts to attend Sunday Mass, to keep the Eucharistic fast, and to abstain from meat on Fridays.
3 Defend the Church when she is denigrated in your presence.

Queenship of the Blessed Virgin Mary

May 31

GOD SPEAKS TO US

He has on His garment and on His thigh a name written: "King of kings and Lord of lords." The Queen takes her place at His right hand, in gold of Ophir.

—Gradual: Apocalypse 19:16 and Psalm 44:10

MEDITATION

The feast of the Queenship of the Blessed Virgin Mary was instituted by Pope Pius XII on October 11, 1954, but already from ancient times we see depictions of Jesus the King beside Mary, who is being crowned by Him.

The Blessed Virgin is therefore a queen. She is one, first of all, by grace: having been created perfect, she is the woman par excellence, the purest woman who has ever existed and will ever exist. From her conception she had such great beauty, such great splendor, such great radiance that she surpasses all the women on earth. "Blessed among women" (Lk. 1:28), she manifested during her life, to an unequalled degree, the greatest natural and supernatural virtues.

Thus she gets her royalty from her original perfection, but she also merited it; she won it by her fiat on the day of the Annunciation, and by her total gift to God which she renewed on Golgotha. While Jesus on Calvary is King, Mary at the foot of the cross is Queen; hence the name "woman" which Jesus gives to her: "Woman, behold your son" (Jn. 19:26). On that day she appeared as the spouse of Our Lord, and as such, she merited the honor and the duty of being mother of the souls that are redeemed by Him. The Blessed Virgin, the spouse of Christ the King, is Queen.

Who are her subjects? She is the Queen of Heaven, gladdening the souls of the elect, the queen of the souls of purgatory, relieving them by her mercy; she is the queen of hell, making herself terrible to the demons, and the queen of angels, apostles, virgins, and of all hearts.

Consequently, she has authority over us. We are her subjects; we should therefore obey her. And so, before making a decision, it is good for us to ask ourselves: what would she do in my position?

As Queen, she desires to protect us and to help us to vanquish the enemies of our souls, as she helped to assure Joan of Arc of victory over her enemies.

While being Queen, she agreed to remain throughout her life "the handmaid of the Lord." She said so on the day of the Annunciation (Lk. 1:38); she repeated it in her *Magnificat* on the day of the Visitation (Lk. 1:48). In this we can imitate her. St. Leo used to say: "To serve God is to reign!"

O Most Blessed Virgin Mary, help us today to imitate you in serving God, so as to merit to reign one day with you in the blessed eternity of Heaven.

Prayer

Grant us, we beseech Thee, O Lord, that we who celebrate the solemnity of the Queenship of the Blessed Virgin Mary may be defended by her protection, and be worthy to obtain peace in the present and glory in the future. Through our Lord, etc. (Collect)

Thoughts

- "Queen by your unique greatness, [O Mary,] you are so by your incomparable power as well."
    —Father Calmel, *365J*, May 31

- "All that the Son asks of the Father is granted to Him. All that the Mother asks of her Son is likewise granted to her."
   —The Curé of Ars, St. John Vianney, *PPJ*, October 12

Resolutions

1. Recite the litanies of the Blessed Virgin while paying special attention to the word "queen." (See Appendix.)
2. Place flowers or a candle in front of a statue or an image of Our Lady.
3. Before making a decision, ask yourself what the Blessed Virgin would do in your position and act accordingly.

St. Angela Merici
June 1

GOD SPEAKS TO US
Behind her the virgins of her train are brought to the King.
—Alleluia: Psalm 44:15

MEDITATION

Angela Merici (1474-1540) was born in Lombardy (Italy) to a deeply Catholic peasant family. Orphaned at the age of fifteen, she was taken in by an uncle who enabled her to complete her religious education. Then a new bereavement, this time of her sister, detached her even more from earthly life and prompted her to join the Third Order of St. Francis. She was moved by the disorders of the world and already showed her compassion for wayward souls. In 1516, she settled in Brescia. Because she loved pilgrimages, she visited several Italian shrines and traveled as far as the Holy Land. On that occasion, she lost her sight during the voyage to the Middle East and regained it only upon her return. The Good Lord thus taught her another form of self-denial. In 1525 she went to Rome, met the Pope there, and then returned to Brescia before taking refuge in Cremona because of the war that was devastating Italy during the reign of Charles V. After peace was declared on August 5, 1529, she returned to Brescia.

Living right in the middle of the Renaissance, she realized that the world around her was becoming pagan and that it was letting itself sink into moral excess. For her there was no doubt that the great remedy for this was the restoration of the Catholic family, and she was aware that in order to bring about this renewal, women, as the educators of the human race, had a key role to play.

Now, by her works of charity, she touched the hearts of many women and girls. They wished to gather together to live in community. However, the saint thought it preferable for them to remain in the world while consecrating their virginity, supported by a strong rule of life. By living in that way, they could be the leaven in the dough and help re-Christianize their country.

In November 1535, assisted by twenty-eight companions, she founded the Ursuline Nuns so as to come to the aid of young girls, especially orphans, spiritually and materially. The order took the form of a monastic rule without cloister, with a minimum of common life for the nuns, in the service of their neighbors. A century later, in France, a rather similar ideal would inspire St. Louise de Marillac, the foundress of the Congregation of the Daughters of Charity.

Attributes

St. Angela is depicted as an Ursuline nun, with a ladder.

Prayer

O God, through Blessed Angela Thou didst cause a new society of consecrated virgins to flourish in Thy Church, grant that we, through her intercession, may live an angelic life, so that, renouncing all earthly joys, we may deserve to enjoy everlasting happiness. Through Jesus Christ. (Collect)

Thoughts

- "There are not two educations, one to make the man and another to make the Christian, but only one for both purposes."

    —Monsignor Louvard, *LP*, 1947

- "Remember that a child's first book is, in reality, the heart of his mother which, when it is imbued with Christian love, dictates to her the lessons appropriate to the age of her pupil."

    —Monsignor Pasquet, *LP*, 1927

Resolutions

1 Recite the Second Joyful Mystery, asking God to raise up holy mothers of families.

2 Support the schools of teaching nuns that provide education for girls.

3 Show great respect for your mother, your sisters, and the women at your workplace.

St. Blandina

June 2

GOD SPEAKS TO US

Though in the sight of men they suffered torments, their hope is full of immortality.

—Wisdom 3:4

MEDITATION

Lyons was evangelized in the second century by St. Pothinus, a disciple of St. Polycarp, Bishop of Smyrna (Asia Minor). A nonagenarian, he endured martyrdom in the year 177 A.D., during the reign of Marcus Aurelius, with forty-seven other Christians including St. Blandina. They underwent the most horrible torments in the municipal amphitheater and in the one belonging to the Gauls. Eusebius, in his Ecclesiastical History (Book V, chapter 1) preserved the account of their martyrdom, comparing them to valiant combatants. The confessors of the faith had only one desire: to meet Jesus in Heaven. They were deeply saddened to see some of their number give up at the terrifying tortures that were inflicted on them, and they feared that others might imitate them.

Among those who held out until the end, Blandina deserves special mention. Here is what Eusebius says about her: "Most violently did the collective madness of the mob, the governor, and the soldiers rage against the holy deacon of Vienna, and against Maturus, a new convert...against Attalus, a native of Pergamus...and against Blandina....For while we were all trembling, [along with] her earthly mistress...lest through the weakness of the flesh she should not be able to profess her faith with sufficient freedom, Blandina was filled with such power, that her ingenious tormentors who relieved and succeeded each other from morning till night, confessed that they were overcome, and had nothing more that they could inflict on her." Blandina was then tied to a stake and exposed to the wild beasts, but not one of them dared to touch her. Then she was taken down from the stake and sent back to prison.

During the next several days, while the other Christians were martyred before her eyes, she was kept until last together with Ponticus, a fifteen-year-old youth. After the latter's death, no one remained but Blandina. "She hastened at last, with joy and exultation, as if she were invited to a marriage feast, and not to be cast to wild beasts. And thus, after scourging, after exposure to the beasts, after roasting, she was finally thrown into a net and cast before a bull, and when she had been well tossed by the animal, and had now no longer any sense of what was done to her by reason of her firm hope, confidence, faith, and her communion with Christ, she too was dispatched." She perished by the sword near the river.

Prayer

Almighty God, who by the preaching of Blessed Pothinus, Thy martyr and bishop, and by the courage of Saint Blandina and her companions, enlightened our fathers who were sitting in darkness and the shadow of death, we pray Thee to grant us the grace to preserve always the memory of such a great favor, and to show unceasingly by our works the faith that we profess. Through Jesus Christ. (Collect)

Thoughts

- "The man who has the good fortune to preserve his patience and meekness is, in this calm, a tangible image of God."
  —The Curé of Ars, St. John Vianney, *PPJ*, August 16

- "To teach with words is good, but example has yet another power over the heart.
  —St. Vincent de Paul, *PPJ*, September 28

RESOLUTIONS

1. Recite the Second Glorious Mystery, asking for the desire for Heaven.
2. Meditate for ten minutes on the sufferings endured by the martyrs and ask God for strength for Christians who are being persecuted today.
3. Call on St. Blandina so that young men and women may have the courage to witness to their faith when the occasion presents itself, without fear of mockery.

St. Clothilde

June 3

God speaks to us

After she had called upon God the Ruler and Savior of all, God changed the king's spirit.

—Alleluia: Esther 15:5, 11

Meditation

Clovis, King of the Franks, suddenly appeared from northern France to extend his reign. He had good relations with St. Remigius, Bishop of Rheims. He respected him and gladly followed his advice. No doubt the holy bishop was the one who advised him to wed Clothilde (†545), a princess from Burgundy, a fervent Catholic who was remarkable for her beauty. After being married in 493 according to the barbarian customs, Clothilde, by her sweetness and charm, little by little won over her husband's heart to the Catholic religion. Their first son died shortly after being baptized; the second, Clodomir, survived thanks to Clothilde's prayers, to the great joy of his parents. A little later, the Alemanni, who looked askance at the extension of the Frankish people and their seizure of the Roman cities, declared war on Clovis. A decisive battle played out in Tolbiac. The defeat of the Franks seemed inevitable. Clovis then exclaimed: "God of Clothilde, if you give me the victory, I will believe in you." And behold, he gained the upper hand over his enemies, cut them to pieces, and routed them. On Christmas Day, 496, faithful to his promise and having been instructed by St. Remigius, he was led to the baptistery in Rheims with three thousand of his warriors. Clothilde's great achievement is to have obtained that grace for him, and thereby to have led his kingdom to Jesus Christ.

After less than twenty years of marriage, Clovis died, having scarcely reached the age of forty-five. He left his wife four sons: Theodoric, whom he had had by his first wife, Clodomir, Childebert, and Clothar, who divided his lands among them. Theodoric took Metz; Clodomir, Orleans;

Childebert, Paris, and Clothar, Soissons. After Clodomir was killed in battle, Clothilde kept in her own home the three children of her late son: Theobald, Gunther, and Clodoald. Fearing that they might seize their father's kingdom, Childbert and Clothar had them put to death by the sword, after deceiving Clothilde by a subterfuge. Then, whereas she had already lost her daughter, Clothar tried to have Childebert killed.

Nevertheless, thanks to Clothilde's persevering prayer at the tomb of St. Martin, Clothar, on the brink of laying hands on his brother, sent him messengers to make peace with him. Nothing more was left for Clothilde to do but to finish her days in prayer and the practice of works of charity until the Divine Master called her.

Prayer

Look favorably, Lord, upon the French nation, and having granted to it the gift of faith, at the pious insistence of Saint Clothilde, give to it now, through her intercession, sincere sentiments of Christian piety. Through Jesus Christ. (Collect)

Thoughts

- "Bow your head, proud Sicamber! Adore what you burned, burn what you adored."
  —St. Remigius to Clovis

- "Learn, my son, that the kingdom of France is predestined by God to defend the Roman Church, which is the only true Church of Jesus Christ. This kingdom will be, someday, great among all the kingdoms. It will be victorious and prosper as long as it is loyal to the Roman faith, but it will be severely chastised every time it is unfaithful to its vocation."
  —St. Remigius to Clovis

Resolutions

1 Recite the Third Glorious Mystery, praying that France may become once again faithful to the promises of her Baptism.

2 Confidently have recourse to prayer in situations that are humanly hopeless.

3 Forgive your enemies from the bottom of your heart and recite an Our Father for their intention.

St. Francis Caracciolo

June 4

GOD SPEAKS TO US

My heart has become like wax melting away within my bosom, because zeal for Your house consumes me.

—Introit: Psalms 21:15 and 68:10

MEDITATION

Born in Villa-Santa-Maria (Kingdom of Naples), Ascanio Caracciolo (1563-1608), loved hunting during his youth, yet already showed great piety. Every day he recited the Little Office of the Blessed Virgin and the Rosary. In order to make sure of his self-control, he resorted to mortification and fled frivolous companions. Moreover he felt a tender compassion for the poor. Nevertheless, he still remained very attached to the world. To help him to separate himself from it, God allowed him suddenly to be afflicted with leprosy, then by cancer of the stomach. Realizing then the vanity of perishable things, he promised God, if he was cured, to devote himself exclusively to Him. His prayer was answered, and he sold all his belongings, entered a confraternity responsible for helping criminals to die in a Christian way, and studied theology.

Ordained a priest in 1588, he founded shortly afterward, with two other companions, the Order of Minor Clerks Regular, whose members pronounce the three vows of religion and also a vow not to seek any office in the Church and not to accept one unless at the explicit request of the Pope. He then took name of Francis. After three years of probation, the Pope approved the new institute, which soon had an abundance of novices. As General of the Order, Francis observed its rules with the utmost exactitude. He fasted, scourged himself, and wore a hair shirt. He introduced his congregation in Spain and founded its first convent in Madrid under the patronage of St. Joseph. Upon returning to Italy, he passed through his native village, where he received a very fine welcome, but he very humbly said to the inhabitants, "I have come to you to make reparation as much as possible for the bad example that I set for you in my youth."

After being reelected Superior General, he got permission to remain in that post for only one year, and after that he became the provost of the Church of St. Mary Major in Naples and the master of novices. God granted him the gift of miracles: he healed the sick and drove out demons. In his preaching, he spoke above all about the love of God. Finally he died, his face beaming with joy, at the age of scarcely forty-five years.

Attribute and patronage

St. Francis Caracciolo is often depicted with a monstrance in his hand. He is the patron of Naples.

Prayer

O God, Thou didst adorn Blessed Francis, the founder of a new Order, with a zeal for prayer and a love of penance; grant that Thy servants may make such progress by imitating him, that by praying unceasingly, and bringing their bodies into subjection, they may be worthy to attain heavenly glory. Through our Lord Jesus Christ…(Collect)

Thoughts

- "You must give yourself to Our Lord in such a way that your heart is His heart, and your life, His life."
  —St. Peter Julian Eymard, *PPJ*, May 29

- "May our only goal be to please Him as much as possible at every moment of our life."
  —Charles de Foucauld, *PPJ*, December 30

Resolutions

1 Recite the Litany of the Sacred Heart. (See Appendix.)

2 In order to lift up your heart more easily to God, limit your use of your cell phone and the internet.

3 Do not aspire to honors, and flee worldliness.

St. Boniface

June 5

God speaks to us

Woe to me if I preach not the Gospel.
—First Epistle of St. Paul to the Corinthians 9:16

Meditation

In the eighth century, apostles like Boniface (680-754) came to mainland Europe from Great Britain; they received their mandate from Rome. Boniface, who at his Baptism received the name of Winfried, was born in England to a distinguished family. Impressed from his earliest youth by the religious who preached missions in his country, he felt the desire to become a monk so as to save souls. Through his formation in a Benedictine monastery, he became erudite and acquired facility in preaching.

Ordained a priest at the age of thirty, he felt the desire to bring the Gospel to faraway places that Providence would show him. He received from Pope Gregory II the mission to evangelize Germany. In May 719 he visited the King of the Lombards, who gave him a very good reception; next he traveled through Bavaria, Thuringia, and then stayed with the Bishop of Utrecht among the Frisians for a three-year period. He spent his time instructing, baptizing, and building churches. He returned to Thuringia, where he brought many pagans to Christianity, then worked among the Hessians, whom he baptized by the thousands. The Pope, satisfied by his ministry, consecrated him a bishop in 723 and gave him the name Boniface (beneficent). Charles Martel, the leader of the Franks, placed him under his protection and recommended him to the bishops, dukes, and counts, so that he came to be respected and esteemed by them all. In Geismar, he cut down an enormous oak tree dedicated to Jupiter, and used the wood to build a chapel in honor of St. Peter. Upon returning to Thuringia, he condemned the bad priests and surrounded himself with young, zealous disciples, among them Sturn, who went on to found

Fulda Abbey. Some holy women came from Great Britain to assist him in his labors. According to his biographer, he converted more than one hundred thousand persons! Elected Bishop of Mainz in 747, he consecrated Pepin the Short in Soissons four years later. Dreaming of new conquests, he turned to Frisia, where he died a martyr, the victim of fanatical pagans, while he was preparing to administer Confirmation to several neophytes.

Saint Boniface, give me an apostolic soul so that I in turn may make known to the souls of those around me God's love for them.

Attributes and patronage

St. Boniface is depicted as a bishop with a hatchet and a felled oak tree at his feet, or holding a book pierced with a sword, but without ruining a single letter. Tailors chose him as their patron so as to be able to use their scissors surely and skillfully.

Prayer

O God, by the zeal of Blessed Boniface, Thy Martyr and Bishop, Thou didst design to call a multitude of peoples to the knowledge of Thy Name; grant, in Thy mercy, that as we keep his feast, so we may also enjoy his protection. Through Our Lord Jesus Christ…(Collect)

Thoughts

- "Let us not be dogs that do not bark, let us not be silent onlookers, let us not be mercenaries who flee at the sight of the wolf, but rather attentive shepherds watching over Christ's flock."

    —St. Boniface

- "Today we need prayer more than ever, if we are to make our apostolic zeal fruitful."

    —St. Peter Julian Eymard, *PPJ*, June 30

Resolutions

1. Offer the Third Glorious Mystery, praying that God may increase the zeal of Catholic missionaries.
2. Write a letter to a non-Catholic friend, or offer him a book to help him draw closer to God.
3. Make a sacrifice so as to obtain the conversion of an unbeliever.

St. Norbert
June 6

God speaks to us

Behold a great priest, who in his days pleased God.
—Gradual: Ecclesiasticus 44:16

Meditation

Norbert (1080-1134), a son of the Count of Gennep (Germany), led a worldly life during his youth. His only ambition was to enjoy life. Although a tonsured cleric and a sub-deacon, he frequented the court, where he was admired for his bearing. Soon he was promoted to the position of chaplain to the Emperor, but in 1115, when he traveled in Westphalia, he was caught in a terrible storm and found himself thrown off his horse, like Saul on the road to Damascus. This fall led him to make a serious examination of conscience and to change his behavior completely. For three years he devoted himself to prayer and mortification; then he was ordained a priest. His first sermon dealt with the vanities of the world of its riches. Teaching not only by his words but also by example, he walked barefoot, clothed in a rough frock that concealed a hair shirt.

God had in store for him the glory of founding a new Order, in Prémontré, near Laon (Aisne): the Order of the Premonstratensians (1120). Its members, religious priests, ministered in parishes while living by the Rule of St. Augustine. Through this way of life, Norbert intended to assure both the renewal of the clergy and the evangelization of the faithful. Nevertheless, the work had scarcely begun when he had to leave the task of continuing it to his successor and disciple, Hugh de Fosse. Indeed, in 1126 he was elevated to the Archiepiscopal See of Magdeburg. At that time, in addition to his heavy responsibility for the spiritual order, the bishop had to address many concerns in the temporal order. Norbert recovered the church properties that were in the hands of the lay princes, and watched especially over the continence of the clergy. Because of this, he did not make many friends, but, supported by divine strength, he managed little by little to remedy the situation. He was backed up in this endeavor by his spiritual sons, whom he had brought to Magdeburg; they helped him in particular to evangelize the northern part of the diocese.

Worn out physically, the saint fell seriously ill in the spring of 1134 and died during the night from June 5 to 6, after having received Viaticum on Pentecost Sunday.

Attribute

St. Norbert's attribute is a monstrance, which he carries in memory of the battle that he waged in Anvers against the heresy of the Sacramentarians.

Prayer

O God, who didst make Blessed Norbert, Thy Confessor and Bishop, an illustrious preacher of Thy word, and through him didst bestow a new offspring upon Thy Church, grant, we beseech Thee, that through his merits and prayers we may be able to practice with Thine aid what he taught both in word and deed. Through our Lord Jesus Christ… (Collect)

Thoughts

- "In all your works, purify your intention, take care to renew it several times a day, repeat often: All for the greater glory of God!"

  —St. Paul of the Cross, *PPJ*, June 29

- "All the saints are witnesses of God inasmuch as, through their good works, God is glorified in the sight of men."

  —St. Thomas Aquinas, *PPJ*, January 8

Resolutions

1 Recite a decade of the Rosary for the priests of your diocese and for missionaries.

2 Keep the Ten Commandments and denounce the invasive attempts to undermine them in the name of "secular values."

3 Act so as to please God and not to make yourself look good.

Ugandan Martyrs

June 7 (celebrated on the 3rd)

GOD SPEAKS TO US

Blessed are they that suffer persecution for justice' sake: for theirs is the kingdom of heaven. Blessed are ye when they shall revile you and persecute you and speak all that is evil against you, untruly, for My sake.

—St. Matthew 5:10-11

MEDITATION

In every age, Catholicism has been persecuted. Every era has had its martyrs. In the late 19th century, in Africa, Uganda had its own. The White Fathers of Cardinal Lavigerie were evangelizing this country. The first Christians there received baptism in 1880 with the support of King Mutesa, but his successor was not equally benevolent toward them. Pressured by the Muslims, the latter feared that the extension of Christianity might be detrimental to the slave trade. Moreover, since he indulged in unnatural practices, he could not bear the exemplary life led by the Christians, so much so that he decided to put to death all those who prayed. A baptized Christian for only a year, Charles Lwanga, the head of the pages, perished by fire at the age of twenty-five. The executioners made the torment last as long as possible. Other adolescents died with him. Wrapped in reeds which were set on fire, they died chanting prayers.

Then Matthias Mulumba, aged fifty, had his turn. They cut off his feet, then his hands, and burned him over a slow fire. Andrew Kagoua, baptized in 1882, displayed great devotion during an epidemic. A zealous soul, he had some influence over the children of the king's minister. The latter was worried about it and decided to have him decapitated. He was thirty years old at the time. Finally, John-Mary—who had been baptized on All Saints Day in 1885 and was very generous to the poor, redeeming the captives whom he evangelized—perished by drowning by order of the minister in January 1887. In all, twenty-two heroes underwent martyrdom. They were at the origin of a flourishing Christendom made up of several hundred thousand baptized souls.

While Pius X introduced the cause for the beatification of Charles Lwanga, Matthias Mulumba and their companions, Benedict XV declared them blessed in 1920, and Paul VI canonized them on October 18, 1964.

Patronage

Charles Lwanga is the patron of African youth.

Prayer

O Lord Jesus Christ, who didst marvelously strengthen the holy martyrs of Uganda, Charles Lwanga, Matthias Mulumba, and all their companions, and who gavest them to us as examples of faith and courage, of chastity, charity, and fidelity, grant, we beseech Thee, that through their intercession the same virtues might increase in us so that we might thus merit to propagate the true faith.

—Prayer, *PS* III, p. 198

Thoughts

- "Our heart cannot be on fire for God and icy cold for men; nor on fire for God and icy cold for God. It is either icy cold or on fire."

    —Charles de Foucauld, *PPJ*, December 5

- "We have as our guarantee these words of our Lord: 'He who loves his life in this world shall lose it, and he who loses it for God shall keep it.'" (cf. Jn. 12:25)

    —St. Francis Xavier, *PPJ*, December 27

Resolutions

1 Recite the Fifth Sorrowful mystery for the Christians in Africa who are victims of persecution.

2 Pray a *Magnificat* in thanksgiving for having received the grace of Baptism. (See Appendix.)

3 Be able to explain clearly to Muslims that belief in the dogma of the Trinity does not imply polytheism.

St. Medard

June 8

God speaks to us

Well done, good and faithful servant, because thou hast been faithful over a few things, I will place thee over many things.

—St. Matthew 25:21

Meditation

Medard (†560) was born in Salency, near Noyon in Picardy (France). He completed his studies in Saint-Quentin.

From his youth he was remarkable for his great charity to the poor. Two facts sufficiently reveal the depths of his soul. One day he met a blind man who was almost naked. Moved with compassion, he took off his own garments so as to clothe him with them, like a new St. Martin. Another time, he ran across thieves who robbed a stranger of his money and fled with his horse. Witnessing the man's distress, he hurried off to his father's stable so as to give him one of the horses there. Heaven then manifested its approval in an unprecedented way. When it started to rain in torrents, an eagle came and hovered over him, covering him with its wings like an umbrella, to the astonishment of his parents and their entourage who saw the miracle.

In order to master perfectly the animal side of his human nature, he allowed his body to have only the food and the sleep that were strictly necessary. He fled worldly gatherings and frequently withdrew at the feet of Jesus in the Sacred Host, where he adored the hidden God for hours. He managed in this way to keep his soul pure and felt the desire for the priesthood awaken in him. Once he was ordained a priest, he edified the faithful by his resplendent virtues: he was pious, humble, charitable, filled with the Good Lord.

At the death of the Bishop of Vermandois, Medard, quite advanced in age, was elected to succeed him. He made use of the situation to have the episcopal see transferred to Noyon, which was easier to defend than Saint-Quentin where he was living. He had the privilege of giving the nun's veil to St. Radegonde, after she left her husband Clothar, who had just assassinated his brother (Prince of Thuringia).

Finally, Medard, a good and faithful servant, departed to gather in Heaven the fruits of his labor. His body was transferred to Soissons, where an abbey was soon built.

Saint Medard, pray to God for me that I may in turn serve Jesus with a generous and charitable heart and thus deserve to sing His mercies eternally.

Invocation

St. Medard is invoked to stop rain and to protect harvests.

Prayer

Almighty God, so wonderful in Thy saints, grant through the merits of Saint Medard that we may be enlightened and strengthened in virtue, and that we, by conforming ourselves to his example and teachings, might love our brethren, practice holiness, and expiate our sins through penance.

—Prayer, *PS*, III, p. 210

Thoughts

- "We must love all men, but we must care more for those whom the world forgets, disdains, rejects: the poor, the little ones, the suffering."
  —Charles de Foucauld, *PPJ*, February 2

- "See Jesus in every human being and act accordingly."
  —Charles de Foucauld, *PPJ*, February 10

Resolutions

1 Recite the Fifth Joyful Mystery for favorable weather at harvest time.

2 Pray five Hail Marys for the bishop of your diocese, that he may give to the souls entrusted to him the spiritual food that they need in order to merit Heaven.

3 Give of your time over the next few days to an aged or infirm person (visit in person or by phone).

Blessed Anna-Maria Taïgi

June 9

GOD SPEAKS TO US

Grace is poured out upon thy lips; therefore hath God blessed thee for ever.

—Offertory: Psalm 44:3

MEDITATION

Although it is true that a great many saints were sanctified in religious life, others climbed the ladder of perfection while living in the world. This was the case with Blessed Anna-Maria Taïgi (1769-1837), an Italian mother of seven children, who sanctified herself by faithfully carrying out her duties as wife and mother of a family.

The daughter of a spendthrift pharmacist and a rude-tempered mother, she learned to read while she was very little, but not to write. As an adolescent, to help her parents who had settled in Rome, she became a chambermaid. At the age of twenty she married Dominic Taïgi, who worked as a laborer at the Chigi Palace. He had a good heart but a short temper. In the evening, upon returning home late, he proved to be very demanding and made life painful for those around him. Anna-Maria took him as he was, striving to tame him by her good nature and sweetness. At the beginning of her marriage, she was a bit flirtatious and led a somewhat worldly life, but after three years of married life, she changed radically. She then received the grace to see above her head something like a sun, topped with a crown of thorns. In this light she discerned God's will. She was thus in permanent contact with Heaven, which made it easier for her to advance along the path of perfection.

In her home, God was served first. Every morning, prayers were recited in common, and in the evening, the recitation of the Rosary while kneeling was followed by a reading from the life of the saint of the day. Anna-Maria watched over her children to make sure that they were always busy. Sometimes she disciplined them with the rod, but more often she punished the recalcitrant ones by imposing a fast (no dinner). She treated herself severely, for example, resolving not to drink at table unless someone explicitly asked her to do so. However she was not lost in spiritual delights. For twenty years she endured the utmost interior dryness, complicated by various ailments: she suffered from headaches, earaches, asthma, bouts of rheumatism, pain in one hand…Despite her ills, she maintained her good sense of humor and was extremely charitable toward her neighbors. At certain times, nevertheless, she enjoyed uncommon spiritual consolations (ecstasies, visions). The household had a lot of financial difficulties, but Anna-Maria, trusting in Providence, always managed to make ends meet. In early June of 1837 she was struck by a fever, and she gave up her soul to God on the ninth of that month, at the age of sixty-eight.

Prayer

Hear our prayer, O God our Savior; grant that, in our joy to celebrate Blessed Anna-Maria Taïgi, we may also be inspired by sentiments of fervent piety. Through Jesus Christ. (Collect)

Thoughts

- "In order to acquire love for God, we must always row against the current and never stop thwarting our own will."

    —Blessed Anna-Maria

- "I entrust myself to my Divine Master. He provides every day for my needs.

    —Blessed Anna-Maria

RESOLUTIONS

1. Call on Blessed Anna-Maria in order to raise the most rambunctious children with firmness and sweetness.
2. Bear patiently with the faults of the family members who are most difficult to get along with.
3. Make a sacrifice so as to draw down God's blessings on your family.

St. Margaret of Scotland

June 10

God speaks to us

The just man hath distributed, he hath given to the poor. His justice remaineth for ever and ever. His horn shall be exalted in glory.

—Psalm 111:9

Meditation

Grand-niece of King St. Edward III, Margaret (1046-1093) was the daughter of Edward and Agatha of Hungary. After spending several years in England, she was compelled, as a result of her father's death, to flee to Scotland with her mother, her brothers, and her sisters. She was twenty-four years old when King Malcolm III, conquered by her charm and her virtues, asked for her hand in marriage. She consented with the intention of thereby promoting the social reign of Our Lord in Scotland, her adopted land. From their union eight children were born: six boys and two girls. Two of them have been raised to the honors of the altars, David and Edith (the future St. Matilda). By her tact and virtue, Margaret tamed the morals of her husband, who was nicknamed "the Bloodthirsty" because he had exterminated the followers of Macbeth. She likewise made use of her authority to restore the Sunday rest, Communion during the Easter season, and the celebration of Mass without the addition of pagan rituals. She also put an end to marriages between close relatives.

Her room was a genuine workshop where she fashioned ornaments. The sacred vessels of the Church of the Holy Trinity, which she commissioned, are made of solid gold, for in her view nothing is too beautiful for the Good Lord. Between the charity that she lavished around her, from morning till evening, and the time that she spent in her pious exercises, it is wonder that twenty-four hours were enough for her to accomplish so many things each day. It is true that she slept very little.

Her charity to the poor is well known. She took care to serve them herself before taking breakfast. And so she does deserve the titles "mother of orphans" and "treasurer of the poor of Jesus Christ." Her biographers report that she used to get up at night to recite the Matins of the Holy Trinity, those of the Cross, of the Blessed Virgin, the Office of the Dead, the hundred fifty psalms followed by Lauds. During the penitential seasons, she heard five or six Masses before attending High Mass.

The Good Lord informed her in advance of the time of her death. She took the opportunity to make a general confession of her life. When her husband died a little before she did, she accepted this difficult separation in atonement for her sins.

Patronage

St. Margaret is the patron of Scotland.

Prayer

O God, who didst make Blessed Queen Margaret a wonderful example of charity to the poor, grant that, by her intercession and example, Thy love may continually grow in our hearts. Through our Lord Jesus Christ…(Collect)

Thoughts

- "In giving itself to God, the heart does not lose its natural tenderness; on the contrary, this tenderness grows and becomes purer and more divine."
    —St. Thérèse of the Child Jesus, *PPJ*, May 8

- "The hand of the poor is the guarantee of the royal treasures: it is a strongbox that the cleverest thieves cannot break into."
    —St. Margaret

Resolutions

1. Be very attentive in reciting the Rosary and in saying your morning and evening prayers, so as to make your prayers more pleasing and more meritorious.
2. Forgive from the bottom of your heart so as to put an end to a stubborn grudge.
3. Do not neglect to offer a tithe so as to provide for the needs of the Church on which we depend.

St. Barnabas

June 11

GOD SPEAKS TO US

The Holy Ghost said to them: Separate [for] Me Saul and Barnabas, for the work whereunto I have taken them.
—Acts of the Apostles 13:2

MEDITATION

Thanks to the Acts of the Apostles, we know a good deal of the life of St. Barnabas (†60). St. Paul describes him as follows: "a Levite, a Cyprian born. Having land, [he] sold it and brought the price and laid it at the feet of the apostles" (Acts 4:36-37).

The lot of St. Barnabas was to a great extent bound up with that of St. Paul. Indeed, when the future Apostle of the Gentiles traveled to Jerusalem, the Christians were not much inclined to welcome him, because of the attitude that he had had toward them before his conversion. Barnabas became his advocate among them: "Barnabas took him and brought him to the apostles and told them how he had seen the Lord, and that He had spoken to him: and how in Damascus he had dealt confidently in the name of Jesus" (Acts 9:27).

At that time, Barnabas departed for Antioch, the capital of Syria, to encourage the new converts. The Holy Ghost then told them that Paul and Barnabas should both set out on a mission (Acts 13:2-3). Their apostolate began on the island of Cyprus and then continued in Asia Minor. They traveled to Antioch, then to Iconium and to Lystra.

During their apostolic journey, the same pattern repeated itself everywhere: whereas well-disposed souls eagerly welcomed them, others showed them hostility; when it reached a critical point, they saw that they were obliged to leave that town. When the Jews resisted grace, "Paul and Barnabas said boldly: 'To you it behoved us first to speak the word of God, but because you reject it and judge yourselves unworthy of eternal life, behold we turn to the Gentiles'" (Acts 13:46).

After a very long voyage, Paul and Barnabas traveled to Jerusalem. There they told St. Peter and the faithful about the fine fruits of the evangelization in the regions that they had visited, and the quarrels that they had had with their opponents during their apostolic expedition (Acts 15:12). Shortly afterward, Paul and Barnabas separated. In Cyprus, the island that was so dear to him, St. Barnabas ended his days, and there he sealed with his blood the Christian faith; various accounts say that he was stoned or burned.

Saint Barnabas, help me, in turn, to carry out an apostolate among well-disposed souls.

Patronage

St. Barnabas is the patron of weavers and tub makers and also of the city of Milan.

Prayer

O God, Thou dost gladden us by the merits and intercession of Blessed Barnabas, Thy Apostle; mercifully grant that we who ask Thy blessings through him may obtain them by the gift of Thy grace. Through our Lord Jesus Christ… (Collect)

Thoughts

- "Let love be without dissimulation, hating that which is evil, cleaving to that which is good."

  —Romans 12:9

- "My beloved brethren, be ye steadfast and unmovable; always abounding in the work of the Lord, knowing that your labour is not in vain in the Lord."

  —I Corinthians 15:58

Resolutions

1. Recite the Fourth Sorrowful Mystery for the Christians of Syria.
2. Read a chapter from the Acts of the Apostles.
3. Be an apostle in your own workplace by your words and example, particularly by your courage in adversity.

St. John of San Facundo

June 12

GOD SPEAKS TO US

Peace I leave with you: My peace I give unto you. Not as the world giveth, do I give unto you.

—St. John 14:27

MEDITATION

Juan González de Castrillo (1430-1479) was born in Spain, in San Facundo. His parents, who for a long time had been childless, begged Our Lady of Pont and their prayers were heard, for they went on to have between seven and nine children. John, the oldest, was raised in a Benedictine monastery, then was welcomed by the Bishop of Burgos into his diocese. Noticing his virtue and especially his charity to the poor, the prelate suggested that he should be ordained a priest. Aware of the requirements of that responsibility, John, in his humility, thought that he was unworthy. Nevertheless, he finally accepted in a spirit of obedience. After the death of his parents, he distributed his belongings to the poor, then traveled to the seminary in Salamanca (1450). Four years later, he lived with a canon for ten years. During that period he taught at the University of Salamanca.

Once he fell seriously ill and received a divine inspiration urging him to enter religious life with the Augustinians. He pronounced his religious vows in 1464, and soon became master of novices, then Assistant Provincial.

In his preaching he did not seek popularity but rather to uproot vices and to plant virtues in souls. At a time when the inhabitants of Salamanca were deeply divided, he tried above all to reconcile hearts. He reminded the lords of their duties, denounced the vice of impurity, and visited prisoners.

A contemplative man, he prolonged his prayer from Matins, which started at one o'clock in the morning, until Lauds, which are chanted at six o'clock. He centered his spiritual life around the Holy Sacrifice of the Mass and the reception of the Holy Eucharist. Feeling unworthy to receive into himself such a holy God, he made a confession several times a day. When he celebrated Holy Mass, he was so enthralled by the beauty of the unfolding mystery that it took him two hours to celebrate it. Occasionally he saw Our Lord, which caused him to have a timeless rapture while celebrating. Moreover he possessed the gift of prophecy and was able to read hearts.

However, his apostolate drew criticism. Indeed, his virtue stirred up the hatred of his adversaries, so that he died poisoned by a woman whom he had rebuked for her misconduct. The inscription on his tomb reads: "Here lies the one to whom Salamanca owes the fact that it is left standing."

Prayer

O God, the author of peace and lover of charity, Thou didst adorn Blessed John, Thy Confessor, with a wonderful grace for reconciling enemies; grant, by his merits and intercession, that, being firmly established in Thy love, no temptation may separate us from Thee. Through our Lord Jesus Christ… (Collect)

Thoughts

- "Holy Communion is the royal wedding of a Christian; it is the visit of the Divine King; it is the Corpus Christi procession of the communicant."
  —St. Peter Julian Eymard, *PPJ*, June 11

- "Be like the bees: they bring nothing into their hives except honey. Let your house be full of sweetness, peace, harmony, humility, and fervor."
  —Padre Pio, *PPJ*, September 8

Resolutions

1 Make a spiritual communion and recite the prayer *Anima Christi*. (See Appendix.)

2 Attend Mass on a weekday.

3 Dare to denounce evil gently but firmly in matters concerning the libertine morals of modern times.

St. Anthony of Padua

June 13

GOD SPEAKS TO US

He that humbleth himself shall be exalted.
—St. Luke 14:11

MEDITATION

The life of St. Anthony (1195-1231)—he was baptized Ferdinand—can be summed up in the Gospel maxim quoted above. Whereas the saintly friar thought only of hiding himself and retreating into his humility, God took pleasure in glorifying him in proportion to his lowliness.

Ferdinand de Bouillon was a descendant, on his father's side, from Godfrey who liberated the Holy Sepulcher. He was born in Lisbon (Portugal) to an illustrious family. When he was five years old he made a vow of virginity. At the age of fifteen, endowed with the charms of youth, handsome, rich, and intelligent, he had every prospect of a fine future in the world. However, disdaining worldly attractions, he withdrew to the Canons Regular of St. Augustine. Since his family kept speaking with him in the parlor, trying to induce him to return to the world, he decided to leave Lisbon to travel to Coimbra. There, the bodies of five Friars Minor who had been martyred in Morocco were interred at his convent. Enthralled by Franciscan life, he decided to be clothed in that habit and took the name of Anthony. In turn he departed for Morocco, longing to shed his blood there for Jesus Christ, but he fell ill on the way and was forced to turn back.

While he was content at the beginning of his religious life to perform manual tasks at his convent, he was asked one day to address a few words to some young, newly ordained clerics. Well, he captivated his audience so much that his superior asked him to prepare to exercise the ministry of preaching. When his formation was completed, he taught in Bologna, Montpellier, Padua, and Toulouse. In Montpellier, one novice, jealous of his success, seized the book on the psalms that he had just finished. The saint was truly upset when he noticed that his work had disappeared. And so he begged God to help him to find it again, and while he was praying, the thief, under the inspiration of the Holy Ghost, came back, very sheepishly admitted his sin, and returned the stolen book to him. Another time, during a solemn procession, after a challenge made by a Jew named Guyard, a mule that had been deprived of food for three days knelt down in the presence of the consecrated Host, paying no attention to the oats that were offered to it.

Soon the hour of reward arrived for the saint. Feeling sick, he had his confreres bring him to Padua, where he breathed his last at the age of thirty-six.

Attributes, invocation, and patronage

St. Anthony is clothed in a Franciscan habit, often with the Child Jesus seated or standing on a book. He is invoked to find lost objects. He is the patron of Portugal.

Prayer

May the votive solemnity of Blessed Anthony, Thy Confessor and Doctor, O God, give joy to Thy Church, that it may always be defended with spiritual aid and be worthy of everlasting joys. Through our Lord Jesus Christ… (Collect)

Thoughts

- "Acts speak louder than words. May your words teach, may your acts speak."

  —St. Anthony

- "Mercy gives the heart compassion for misery, drives all hardness out of the heart, and floods the heart with an admirable sweetness."

  —St. Anthony, Sermon XXII after Trinity

Resolutions

1 Call on St. Anthony when someone has lost an object, and do not neglect to thank him once it has been found.

2 Ask yourself about your vocation and do not shirk it.

3 Be gentle in your relations with others.

St. Basil the Great

June 14

GOD SPEAKS TO US

My faithfulness and My kindness shall be with him, and through My name shall his horn be exalted.

—Offertory: Psalm 88:25

MEDITATION

Basil (ca. 330-379) was born in Caesarea, Cappadocia in a family with ten children. In Athens he studied literature, history, and the sciences, without neglecting Sacred Scripture and the Fathers of the Church. He started to teach in Caesarea, then made a tour of the monasteries in the Near East and in Egypt. Returning then to his country, he withdrew to Pontus. He ate very frugally, slept very little, and joined prayer with intellectual and manual work. He savored the tranquility and calm of a life away from the world and completely oriented toward God. Soon disciples crowded around him. For them he composed the Great Rules and the Little Rules which contain wise instruction and advice.

Around the year 362, he was summoned to receive priestly ordination, which he accepted somewhat fearfully, and then in 370 he was elevated to the episcopate. As Bishop of Caesarea, he had to confront the Arian Emperor Valens, a man with a harsh, defiant character and limited intelligence. His prefect, Modestus, had the task of preparing for him a favorable welcome from Basil. He engaged in the following memorable conversation with the bishop. "Is it true, Basil, that you refuse to adhere to the religious faith of the Emperor?" "In matters of faith," Basil replied, "I owe obedience to an Emperor more powerful than the majesties of this earth. God forbids me to adore a creature. Now you take blasphemy to the point of claiming that Jesus Christ is only a creature." "Now there you insult us!" the prefect continued. "Does our authority mean nothing to you?" "What makes a Christian is not the nobility of persons or of titles, but the purity of the faith." "What?! You do not fear my authority?" "Why should I fear it?" "I can confiscate your property, exile you, torture you, or put you to death." "Tell me some other punishments; none of these frightens me. You can confiscate nothing from a man who possesses nothing; I am not attached to any fatherland; my very weak body will not withstand the first torture, and death would be a priceless benefit to me; it would lead me instantly to the God whom I serve." "Never has anyone spoken to me in this way!" "Perhaps because you never met a bishop, for any bishop would have shown the same independence in matters of the faith." The prefect had to admit that he was beaten.

The saintly bishop, whose health was so precarious, died after saying, "Lord, into Your hands I commend my spirit."

Prayer

Hear our prayers, we beseech Thee, O Lord, which we offer on the feast of Blessed Basil, Thy Confessor and Bishop, and by the interceding merits of him who was found worthy to serve Thee well, absolve us from all our sins. Through our Lord Jesus Christ... (Collect)

Thoughts

- "There is only one method to follow in order to acquaint oneself with perfection: meditations on the divinely inspired Scriptures. There we find rules for conduct."

  —St. Basil, Letter to St. Gregory Nazianzen

- "Anyone who tries to become perfect in all sorts of virtues must study the lives of the saints, as so many living, practical models, and then, by diligent imitation, make his own the good that is found in them."

  —St. Basil

Resolutions

1. Recite an Act of Faith. (See Appendix.)
2. Be uncompromising with error, while avoiding fruitless criticism and ill will at home, at your workplace, etc.
3. Read a chapter of the New Testament, or the Gospel for the day.

St. Germaine

June 15

God speaks to us

God hath exalted the humble.

—St. Luke 1:52

Meditation

Because He is great, God has a preferential love for the humble. A humble man, from the depths of his nothingness, adores God, the principle of all good, and expresses to Him his gratitude for it. Privations do not affect him, because he has set his heart on treasure elsewhere. He expects his reward from God alone. St. Germaine of Pibrac (1579-1601), without having studied, put into practice the principles of humility. The daughter of a poor farmer and a devout mother, she had a crippled right hand and was afflicted with skin ulcers. When she was still very young, her mother died and her father remarried a woman who took a dislike to her. She consoled herself by living close to the Good Lord as a shepherdess, in the green countryside, in the midst of flowers and birds, steeped in the chief truths of the faith that she had learned from her parish priests in catechism class. One winter day, when she was getting ready to give bread to some poor people, her stepmother rushed over to strike her, but when Germaine opened her apron, it was filled with fresh, fragrant flowers, tied into a bouquet.

The science of love imparted to her the science of duty. Since she loved Jesus with her whole heart, she found great joy in receiving Him in Holy Communion. In order to make herself less unworthy, she went to Confession every week. It happened on occasion that her guardian angel watched over the sheep in her place for the duration of the Mass. She had a tender devotion to Our Lady, which she maintained by reciting the Rosary and the Angelus, and which she intensified on each of her feast days. Thus her solitary life was spent in the utmost self-effacement.

God tests those whom He loves, and Germaine was not

spared. Her infirmity already led her to be neglected and disdained, even in her own family. Although she witnessed the caresses lavished on her brothers and sisters, she was deprived of them and relegated to a corner, condemned to sleep under a staircase. She accepted these inconveniences with admirable patience.

One morning she was found dead on her bed of straw; she was only twenty-two years old. Her body was found intact, forty years later, and many graces have been granted since then through her intercession.

O Saint Germaine, model of humility and patience in adversity, intercede for me that I may in turn practice all these virtues that are so pleasing to God.

Invocation

St. Germaine is invoked against ailments of the eyes.

Prayer

O God, who art the greatness of the humble and didst will that Blessed Germaine should shine with all the splendor of charity and patience, grant through her merits and intercession that, by carrying our cross constantly, we might love Thee constantly. Through our Lord Jesus Christ... (Collect)

Thoughts

- "In an age in which the whole world runs after fortune, pleasure, and honors, nothing is more necessary than to propose for our admiration and our imitation a life that is sanctified in poverty, suffering, and contempt."
  —Pius IX, in *ACP*

- "A world that has been led astray by vain systems of philosophy and science must be counteracted by the true wisdom and true science that Germaine had learned at the foot of the cross.
  —Pius IX, in *ACP*

Resolutions

1. Recite the Litany of Humility. (See Appendix.)
2. Avoid calling attention to yourself.
3. Accept being shunned by others.

St. John Francis Regis

June 16

GOD SPEAKS TO US

That which you hear in the ear, preach ye upon the house tops.
—St. Matthew 10:27

MEDITATION

Born in Fontcouverte (today in the Aude region) in a deeply Catholic family, John Francis Régis (1597-1640) was very pious from his childhood. He was sickly and once on the point of death, but he was cured suddenly, and then made a vow to devote himself forever to the salvation of souls. At the age of nineteen he entered the Jesuit community in Toulouse, then was ordained a priest in 1630. He performed his first ministry in his native parish. He loved with a special love the poor and souls that had gone astray. His apostolic success led his superiors to employ him solely in the preaching ministry. He touched souls by addressing them in language that was simple yet anointed with profound conviction. His apostolic career lasted only ten years, but that was enough time to reawaken piety and virtue in Languedoc, Vivarais, and Velay, regions which at that time were devastated by the Calvinist heresy and the corruption of morals. He traveled from one mountainous site to another in all kinds of weather, clothed in a hair shirt, most often being content with bread and water for his food, and very little sleep.

Given such great virtues, combined with so many miraculous conversions, hell was unleashed against him. The Bishop of Viviers reproached him for his excessive zeal, but the saint did not try to justify himself at all, admitting his modest intelligence.

God rewarded his virtue by lavishing upon him the gift of miracles. When a poor woman asked him to repair her tattered cloak, the saint complied. Shortly afterward, the two children of that woman, who were seriously ill, found themselves cured as soon as they were covered by the cloak.

In a time of famine, he gave the poor their fill of grain, thanks to the storehouse that he owned in Puy, which he supplied by calling on the rich people of the region. Now several times the storehouse was filled miraculously, to the great astonishment of the manager, Marguerite Baud. The saint also possessed the gift of prophecy. He told a young man who was thinking about marriage that he would enter the Society of Jesus, which then happened. A man who had been possessed for eight years was delivered by a simple sign of the cross, whereas a number of exorcists had failed to liberate him. In 1640, Francis Regis died a very holy death in La Louvesc after saying: "I die content; I see Jesus and Mary who deign to come before me to lead me into Paradise."

Prayer

O God who, in view of the immense labors that he would have to bear for the salvation of souls, didst endow Blessed John Francis with wondrous charity and patience in every trial, grant to us, in Thy goodness, that instructed by his example and aided by his intercession, we might deserve the rewards of eternal life. Through Jesus Christ… (Collect)

Thoughts

- "Ask God for the disposition to be quite willing to give your life for Jesus Christ."
  —St. Vincent de Paul, *PPJ*, April 28

- "The greatest sentiments of Our Lord were [directed toward] caring for the poor so as to cure them, to console them, to help them, and to advise them. That was what He loved."
  —St. Vincent de Paul, *PPJ*, May 12

Resolutions

1 Recite the Litany of the Sacred Heart. (See Appendix.)

2 Say a decade of the Rosary, asking God to raise up missionaries in your country.

3 Perform some thankless task in your household or your family.

St. Gregory Barbarigo

June 17

God speaks to us

Here is the faithful and wise steward, whom his lord setteth over his family, to give them their measure of wheat in due season.

—Communion: St. Luke 12:42

Meditation

Gregory Barbarigo (1625-1697) was born in Venice in an illustrious family. A diplomat at the age of twenty, he was sent to assist Ambassador Contarini in preparing the Treaty of Westphalia in 1648, which put an end to the Thirty Years War. Upon his return, he entered the clergy, then in 1655 became a doctor in canon law and civil law. Two years later, he was consecrated Bishop of Bergamo. There he applied the instructions of the Council of Trent, taking Charles Borromeo as his example. When he became Bishop of Padua in 1664, he did not think it too insignificant to teach catechism himself to little children, nor to preside in person at the monthly conferences of the priests dealing with "cases of conscience" so as to help them to resolve the difficulties that they encountered in their apostolate.

Aware of the importance of the formative years of young people for the future of both the Church and of society, he opened hundreds of schools and founded a seminary endowed with an extensive library, which was in particular had many volumes on Sacred Scripture and the works of the Fathers of the Church. There he developed university chairs in Oriental languages and a polyglot printing house. His great erudition enabled him to gain considerable influence over the students.

He made use of his large inheritance to help the poor and to ensure the development of the charitable works of his diocese, while living himself in extreme poverty. His clothing was sometimes quite worn out, and he went so far as to sell off his furniture, including his own bed.

The secret of his detachment from worldly goods and

of the abundance of his good works should be sought in his life of union with God. He was above all a man of prayer. The flourishing of his diocese was not his only intention. St. Gregory had a much wider heart, which led him to pray for the union of the Eastern and Western Churches, and also for the conversion of Jews and pagans. At the death of Innocent XI in 1689, learning that some cardinals ardently wished to elect him Pope, he campaigned for Pietro Ottoboni, who was elected and took the name Alexander VIII. As for him, he died on June 18, 1697, at the age of seventy-two. His body was found intact twenty-eight years later.

Prayer

O God, who willed that Blessed Gregory, Thy Bishop and Confessor, should shine by his pastoral solicitude and compassion for the poor, grant, in Thy mercy, that while celebrating his merits we might also imitate his example of charity. Through Jesus Christ… (Collect)

Thoughts

- "After His divine preaching, Jesus used to withdraw alone on the mountain to pray. The congregation rests on a foundation like this. And if that is torn down, then the building is totally ruined, because then the work is completely outside of the vocation that God gave me."
—St. Paul of the Cross, *PPJ*, September 16

- "I recommend in particular that you keep yourselves in the presence of God, not by a dry, sterile effort, but rather in an affectionate, peaceful, calm way, so as to be penetrated by His Spirit."
—St. Paul of the Cross, *PPJ*, December 20

Resolutions

1 Recite an Act of Charity. (See Appendix.)

2 Read a chapter from a book on doctrine or the catechism.

3 Respect your superiors in word and deed; pray for them.

St. Ephrem

June 18

GOD SPEAKS TO US

The just man shall flourish like the palm tree; like a cedar of Lebanon shall he grow.

—Offertory: Psalm 91:13

MEDITATION

Ephrem (306-373) was born in Nisibis, a Roman province in Mesopotamia. His father, a priest of the god Abnil, expelled him from his home because of his attachment to Christianity. He was taken in by St. James (303-388), the local bishop, who gave him a solid formation that was both intellectual and spiritual. Baptized at the age of eighteen, he started by working in the public baths, then at the advice of a monk he left the world to retire to the desert.

During the wars that pitted the Romans against the Persians (338-387), Ephrem learned that Christians in his native place were enduring terrible persecutions. He returned then to Nisibis to support them. Thanks to his prayers and those of his bishop, the city, which was under siege by Sapor II, King of the Persians, was liberated (338). Hoping to assist the famished inhabitants, Ephrem was elevated to the diaconate in order to carry out that responsibility, but refused the priesthood out of humility.

When Nisibis fell into the power of the Persians, Ephrem took refuge in Edessa, where he spent the last ten years of his life. During that period he composed most of his works. We owe him in particular several priceless commentaries on Sacred Scripture; Pope Benedict XV ranked him almost at the same level as St. Jerome. He was the author of other works dealing with the primacy of Peter, the presence of Jesus in the Eucharist, original sin, and the two natures of Jesus Christ.

In his writings, St. Ephrem also manifests a great love for the Blessed Virgin. He exalts her virginity, her universal mediation, and her Immaculate Conception. Since poetry was prized highly by the Gnostics, he composed in verse homilies which are so remarkable that he was nicknamed "The Lyre of the Holy Ghost."

The portrait that he sketches of a bishop perfectly sums up his own virtues: "kind, pure, virginal, wise, serious, poor, cultivated, temperate, self-controlled." His prayers and his speeches were often accompanied by tears.

Pope Benedict XV declared him a Doctor of the Church.

Prayer

O God, who didst will to enlighten Thy Church by the wondrous learning and glorious merits of Blessed Ephrem, Thy Confessor and Doctor, we humbly beseech Thee, to defend her by his intercession and Thy continual power against the snares of false teaching and iniquity. Through our Lord Jesus Christ… (Collect)

Thoughts

- "When a man does penance, a drop of [divine] mercy wipes away the seal imprinted on his soul by his sins."
  —St. Ephrem, *De Ecclesia*, V, 16, p. 614d

- "When we have overcome our passions, destroyed within us all natural, disordered affections, and emptied our mind of all preoccupations that are useless for salvation, then the Holy Ghost, finding our soul at rest, will put light into our hearts, as one lights a lamp that is already supplied with a wick and oil.
  —St. Ephrem

Resolutions

1 Recite a prayer to the Holy Ghost so as to draw God's blessings down upon us.

2 Make a sacrifice in order to show your regret for your sins.

3 Practice one of the virtues mentioned at the end of the meditation.

St. Juliana Falconieri

June 19

GOD SPEAKS TO US

Now there stood by the cross of Jesus his mother and his mother's sister, Mary of Cleophas, and Mary Magdalene.
—St. John 19:25

MEDITATION

Juliana Falconiere (1270-1341) was born in Florence (Italy) of parents who were already advanced in age. Her father died soon afterward, so an uncle took charge of her education. Jesus and Mary were the first two words that she pronounced. At the age of fourteen she was the first to receive the habit of the Third Order Servites, from the hands of St. Philip Beniti. She made her profession the following year, shortly before the death of the saintly religious, and thereby found herself at the head of the fledgling congregation.

Very austere in her own practices, she dedicated Mondays to relieving the souls in purgatory, adding penances to her prayers and taking the discipline. She dedicated Fridays to meditation on the Passion of Our Lord, while scourging herself until she drew blood, and on Saturdays she contemplated the sorrows of Our Lady at the foot of the cross. On Wednesdays and Fridays she was fed by the Holy Eucharist, and on Saturday, she was content with bread and water. She slept very little, spending most of her time in prayer.

In 1304 the Order was officially recognized by a Bull written by Pope Benedict XI. Two years later, she agreed to be the Superior of it at the explicit request of the General of the Order, the successor of St. Philip. That did not prevent her from seeking the humblest tasks, such as caring for patients with the most repugnant illnesses. She did good to all. In Florence, she was an instrument of peace, managing to reconcile feuding families. Moreover she relieved the poor and cured the sick by a simple sign of the cross. Confronted with such great virtues, the devil sought his revenge. Indeed she had to undergo painful temptations, but she overcame them valiantly by drawing strength from prayer. Her austerities finally ruined her health. A stomach illness, which she had contracted long before, prevented her from receiving the Holy Eucharist in the last moments of her life. Feeling that her end was near, she asked her confessor to set the Sacred Host on a corporal and to place it on her chest. The Host then disappeared and the saint took her final breath while saying, "My sweet Jesus."

As they were preparing her for burial, her sisters discerned over her heart the sacred imprint of the Host, with the image of Jesus crucified. They also found around her waist an iron belt that was embedded in her flesh. In memory of the Eucharistic miracle, the nuns of the Order of Servites wear today an image of a host on their scapular.

Prayer

O God, who didst deign wondrously to refresh Blessed Juliana, Thy Virgin, in her last sufferings with the precious Body of Thy Son, grant, we beseech Thee, that, by her intercession and merits, we also, refreshed and strengthened by the same sacrament in the agony of death, may be brought to our heavenly country. Through the same Jesus Christ… (Collect)

Thoughts

- "Make a meditation on the Passion of the Redeemer before leaving your room, and you will see that everything will go well and that you will live far from sin."
  —St. Paul of the Cross, *PPJ*, March 15

- "Meditate often on the sorrows of the Mother of God, sufferings that are inseparable from those of her beloved Son."
  —St. Paul of the Cross, *PPJ*, October 1

Resolutions

1 Contemplate for ten minutes Mary at the foot of the cross.
2 Say a prayer for the benefit of the souls in purgatory and offer a mortification to relieve them.
3 Straighten up your room.

St. Alban

June 20 (celebrated on the 22nd)

God speaks to us

Wisdom conducted the just through the right ways and showed him the kingdom of God.

—Wisdom 10:10

Meditation

A terrible persecution was raging in Gaul and in Great Britain early in the reign of Diocletian, under the influence of Maximian who governed in the West. One of the noblest victims in Great Britain was St. Alban, an upright man in search of the truth. God would lead him to the heroic faith and charity that he manifested during his martyrdom.

Alban (†287), a rich, intelligent young man who was eager to learn, traveled to Rome to increase his intellectual and moral heritage. When he did not find what he was seeking, he returned to England and settled in Verulam, near London. A charitable man, he welcomed the poor people who turned to him. One day, without knowing it, he offered hospitality to a Catholic priest who was fleeing the persecution. He was struck by his patience and even by the radiant joy on his face; seeing him spend long hours in prayer, he asked him the reason for it. The priest then revealed to him his identity and gave him his first catechism lessons. For the moment Alban was still perplexed. He felt drawn by the truth, but it was difficult for him to adhere to it, for he knew that Christianity was condemned by the law, and he hesitated. He said to himself: if I obey God, I will have to sacrifice my fortune, but if I disobey him, I will sacrifice my soul, and with it my eternity. To help him to resolve the dilemma, Our Lord appeared to him in a dream, nailed to the cross, then risen and ascending into Heaven. The next day the priest explained to him the meaning of his vision and the need to believe in the Father, the Son, and the Holy Ghost.

Alban then made such a fine act of faith that the priest

baptized him immediately. The devil, furious at losing his prey, sought an opportunity for revenge. An idolater, noticing the presence of a stranger in Alban's house, denounced him to the magistrate. In order to save the priest, Alban then exchanged clothing with him. The next day, soldiers invaded the house and demanded, in the name of the law, that he hand the stranger over to them. Alban, wearing the priest's coat, refused to tell them where he was, and declared himself a Christian. That was enough to turn their fury against him. They beat him, then threw him into prison where he remained for six months. It was a time of severe drought, and the people saw this as punishment from God, so that Alban was set free. But far from rejoicing, he was saddened at the thought of missing martyrdom.

Finally he witnessed openly to his faith, which incited the pagans to condemn him for good. A soldier cut off his head. The work of God was accomplished: Alban was led into heaven.

Attributes and invocation

St. Alban is depicted decapitated with his head in his hands, placed on the Gospel book. He is invoked against headaches.

Prayer

Almighty God, grant to us who celebrate the birth in Heaven of Blessed Alban, Thy martyr the grace to be, by his intercession, strengthened in the love of your name. Through Jesus Christ… (Collect)

Thoughts

- "I know that God accomplishes His purpose with strength, but that He disposes all things gently."
  —Pauline Jaricot, *PPJ*, September 11
- "Love is proved through suffering."
  —Pauline Jaricot, *PPJ*, September 6

Resolutions

1 Recite a *Magnificat* to thank God for your Baptism.
2 Help a priest by your prayers or your services.
3 Witness to the faith at the next opportunity.

St. Aloysius of Gonzaga

June 21

GOD SPEAKS TO US

Blessed are the clean of heart: for they shall see God.
—St. Matthew 5:8

MEDITATION

No virtue is exalted as much in Sacred Scripture as purity. The finest praise that Our Lord bestowed on it was His decision to be born of a Virgin Mother. Afterwards, He adorned the Church, his Mystical Bride, with the most resplendent jewel of virginity. In Heaven, moreover, the saints in the highest places are the ones whose victory was most brilliant, because it was purchased at the price of heroic struggles. One of them is Aloysius of Gonzaga (1568-1591), born in Mantua, Italy, a descendant of two families that had given the Church cardinals and popes. Since he was of noble birth—his father was an Imperial Prince, and his mother was a lady of honor serving Isabelle of France, the wife of Philip II—he therefore had to safeguard his purity not in the solitude of retreats, but rather in the midst of the schemes and temptations of court. Moreover, he had received from Heaven a fine intellect and sound judgment, and had learned the art of good manners. Would he escape from the brilliant career ahead of him? For his father, there was no doubt that Aloysius would join the military. He clothed him in a uniform at a very young age and took him among soldiers. There, young Aloysius learned words that were too daring, which he innocently repeated. When corrected, he bitterly regretted what he later called "the sins of his youth" but derived from the experience a greater mistrust of himself, a portent of his future victories. In fact, he rapidly progressed in the practice of virtues, relying on the Blessed Virgin whom he dearly loved. Reading a book on the Mysteries of the Rosary did him much good and inspired in him the desire to consecrate his virginity to Our Lady so as to imitate her purity.

To achieve this, Aloysius frequently confessed his sins and soon prepared for his First Communion, which he received from the hands of St. Charles Borromeo. Frequent reception of the Holy Eucharist mightily helped him to increase in virtue. Another way of safeguarding his innocence was by custody of the eyes: he kept his eyes lowered when in the street, avoiding any source of temptation. He further subdued his flesh with strict abstinence and tough discipline. Seeing all his efforts, God rewarded him by giving him tangible signs of His presence. He joined the Jesuits in 1585, but would experience religious life for only a few years. The divine love that consumed him detached him totally from the earth and made him worthy, after a short illness, of the beatific vision.

Attributes and patronage

St. Aloysius is represented with a large surplice, holding a crucifix in his hand. He is the patron saint of youth and of Mantua.

Prayer

O God, the giver of heavenly gifts, in the angelic youth Aloysius Thou didst unite a wonderful innocence with an equal spirit of penance. Through his merits and prayers grant that we, who have not followed him in his innocence, may imitate him in his penance. Through our Lord… (Collect)

Thoughts

- "He who fails to help his neighbor's soul knows not how to love God, for he does not seek to increase His glory."
  —Maxim of St. Aloysius de Gonzaga

- "Do not presume on your strength."
  —St. Benedict, *PPJ*, August 23

RESOLUTIONS

1. Recite three Hail Marys to ask the Blessed Virgin for the grace of purity.
2. Keep your eyes lowered when going from one place to another.
3. Make reparation for each sin of impurity by a sacrifice.

Prayers

Spiritual Communion

Spiritual communion consists in an ardent desire to receive Jesus in the Host, and in an act of love such as one would make if one had received Him sacramentally.[13] The Council of Trent strongly praises spiritual communion and encourages the faithful to practice it.[14]

To make a good spiritual communion, St. Alphonsus Liguori recommends the following act:

> My Jesus, I believe that Thou art Present in the Blessed Sacrament. I Love Thee above all things, and I desire Thee in my Soul. Since I cannot now receive Thee sacramentally, come at least spiritually into my heart. As though Thou wert already there, I embrace Thee and unite myself wholly to Thee; permit not that I should ever be separated from Thee.[15]

Depending on the circumstances, if one needs a shorter prayer, or if one prefers a simpler form, the same saint proposes that we very simply say:

> O Jesus, I believe that You are present in the Blessed Sacrament; I love You and desire You. Come into my heart. I embrace You. Please never leave me.[16]

---

[13] St. Thomas Aquinas, *Summa Theologica*, IIIa, q. 80, a. 1, *ad* 3.
[14] Council of Trent, Session XIII, Decree Concerning the Sacrament of the Eucharist, ch. 8, in DZ 1648-1649.
[15] St. Alphonsus Liguori, *Visits to the Blessed Sacrament*, Apôtre du Foyer, 2000, p. 26.
[16] *Ibid.*, p. 27.

The Mysteries of the Rosary

Joyful Mysteries

First Mystery: The Annunciation by the Angel Gabriel to the Virgin Mary; intention for this mystery: humility.

Second Mystery: The Visitation of Our Lady to her cousin Elizabeth; intention for this mystery: fraternal charity.

Third Mystery: The Birth of Jesus in a stable; intention for this mystery: the spirit of poverty.

Fourth Mystery: The Presentation of the Child Jesus in the Temple: intention for this mystery: obedience and purity.

Fifth Mystery: The Finding of the Child Jesus in the Temple: intention for this mystery: to seek God in everything.

Sorrowful Mysteries

First Mystery: The Agony of Jesus in the Garden of Olives; intention for this mystery: contrition for our sins.

Second Mystery: The Scourging of Our Lord; intention for this mystery: mortification of the senses.

Third Mystery: The Crowning with Thorns; intention for this mystery: mortification of the mind and heart.

Fourth Mystery: The Carrying of the Cross: intention for this mystery: patience and perseverance in trials.

Fifth Mystery: The Crucifixion and Death of Jesus on the Cross: intention for this mystery: greater love for God and for souls.

Glorious Mysteries

First Mystery: The Resurrection of Our Lord; intention for this mystery: faith.

Second Mystery: The Ascension of Jesus into heaven; intention for this mystery: hope.

Third Mystery: The Descent of the Holy Ghost on the Blessed Virgin and the Apostles; intention for this mystery: missionary zeal.

Fourth Mystery: The Assumption of Our Lady into heaven: intention for this mystery: the grace of a happy death.

Fifth Mystery: The Coronation of Mary as Queen of Heaven: intention for this mystery: greater devotion to the Blessed Virgin.

The Apostles' Creed

I believe in God, the Father Almighty, Creator of heaven and earth;

and in Jesus Christ, His only Son, Our Lord,

Who was conceived by the Holy Ghost, born of the Virgin Mary,

suffered under Pontius Pilate, was crucified, died, and was buried.

He descended into hell; the third day He rose again from the dead;

He ascended into heaven, and sitteth at the right hand of God, the Father Almighty,

from thence He shall come to judge the living and the dead.

I believe in the Holy Ghost,

the holy Catholic Church, the communion of saints,

the forgiveness of sins,

the resurrection of the body,

and life everlasting. Amen.

An Act of Faith

O my God, I firmly believe that Thou art One God in Three Divine Persons: Father, Son, and Holy Ghost. I believe that Thy Divine Son became man and died for our sins, and that He shall come to judge the living and the dead. I believe these and all the truths which the Holy Catholic Church teaches because Thou hast revealed them, Who canst neither deceive nor be deceived.

An Act of Hope

O my God, relying on Thy almighty power and infinite mercy and promises, I hope to obtain pardon of my sins, the help of Thy grace, and life everlasting, through the merits of Jesus Christ, my Lord and Redeemer.

An Act of Charity

O my God, I love Thee above all things, with my whole heart and soul, because Thou art all-good and worthy of all love. I love my neighbor as myself for the love of Thee. I forgive all who have injured me and ask pardon of all whom I have injured.

An Act of Contrition

O my God, I am heartily sorry for having offended Thee, and I detest all my sins, because I dread the loss of heaven and the pains of hell, but most of all because I have offended Thee, my God, who art all good and deserving of all my love. I firmly resolve, with the help of Thy grace, to confess my sins, to do penance, and to amend my life. Amen.

Memorare

Remember, O most gracious Virgin Mary, that never was it known that anyone who fled to thy protection, implored thy help, or sought thy intercession, was left unaided. Inspired by this confidence, I fly unto thee, O Virgin of virgins, my Mother. To thee do I come, before thee I stand, sinful and sorrowful.

O Mother of the Word Incarnate, despise not my petitions, but in thy mercy hear and answer me. Amen.

Litany of the Sacred Heart

Lord, have mercy. *Lord, have mercy.*
Christ, have mercy. *Christ, have mercy.*
Lord, have mercy. *Lord, have mercy.*
Christ, hear us. *Christ, hear us.*
Christ, graciously hear us. *Christ, graciously hear us.*
God the Father of heaven, *have mercy on us.*
God the Son, Redeemer of the world,
God the Holy Ghost,
Holy Trinity, one God,
Heart of Jesus, Son of the Eternal Father,
Heart of Jesus, formed by the Holy Ghost in the womb of the Virgin Mother,
Heart of Jesus, substantially united to the Word of God,
Heart of Jesus, of Infinite Majesty.
Heart of Jesus, sacred Temple of God,
Heart of Jesus, Tabernacle of the Most High,
Heart of Jesus, House of God and Gate of heaven,
Heart of Jesus, burning furnace of charity,
Heart of Jesus, abode of justice and love,
Heart of Jesus, full of goodness and love,
Heart of Jesus, abyss of all virtues,
Heart of Jesus, most worthy of all praise,

Litany of the Sacred Heart

Heart of Jesus, King and center of all hearts,
Heart of Jesus, in whom are all treasures of wisdom and knowledge,
Heart of Jesus, in whom dwells the fullness of divinity,
Heart of Jesus, in whom the Father was well pleased,
Heart of Jesus, of whose fullness we have all received,
Heart of Jesus, desire of the everlasting hills,
Heart of Jesus, patient and most merciful,
Heart of Jesus, enriching all who invoke Thee,
Heart of Jesus, fountain of life and holiness,
Heart of Jesus, propitiation for our sins,
Heart of Jesus, loaded down with opprobrium,
Heart of Jesus, bruised for our offenses,
Heart of Jesus, obedient to death,
Heart of Jesus, pierced with a lance,
Heart of Jesus, source of all consolation,
Heart of Jesus, our life and resurrection,
Heart of Jesus, our peace and our reconciliation,
Heart of Jesus, victim for our sins,
Heart of Jesus, salvation of those who trust in Thee,
Heart of Jesus, hope of those who die in Thee,
Heart of Jesus, delight of all the Saints,
Lamb of God, who takest away the sins of the world, *spare us, O Lord.*
Lamb of God, who takest away the sins of the world, *graciously hear us, O Lord.*
Lamb of God, who takest away the sins of the world, *have mercy on us, O Lord.*

V. Jesus, meek and humble of heart,
R. Make our hearts like unto Thine.

Let us pray: Almighty and eternal God, look upon the Heart of Thy most beloved Son and upon the praises and satisfaction which He offers Thee in the name of sinners; and to those who implore Thy mercy, in Thy great goodness, grant forgiveness in the name of the same Jesus Christ, Thy Son, who liveth and reigneth with Thee forever and ever. Amen.

Litany of the Blessed Virgin

(Litany of Loreto)

Lord, have mercy. *Lord, have mercy.*
Christ, have mercy. *Christ, have mercy.*
Lord, have mercy. *Lord, have mercy.*
Christ, hear us. *Christ, graciously hear us.*
God, the Father of Heaven, *have mercy on us.*
God the Son, Redeemer of the World, *have mercy on us.*
God the Holy Spirit, *have mercy on us.*
Holy Trinity, One God, *have mercy on us.*
Holy Mary, *pray for us.*
Holy Mother of God,
Holy Virgin of Virgins,
Mother of Christ,
Mother of Divine Grace,
Mother of the Church,
Mother most Pure,
Mother most Chaste,
Mother Inviolate,
Mother Undefiled,
Mother most Amiable,
Mother most Admirable,
Mother of good Counsel,
Mother of our Creator,
Mother of our Savior,
Virgin most Prudent,
Virgin most Venerable,
Virgin most Renowned,
Virgin most Powerful,
Virgin most Merciful,
Virgin most Faithful,
Mirror of Justice,
Seat of Wisdom,
Cause of our Joy,
Spiritual Vessel,

Litany of the Blessed Virgin

Vessel of Honor,
Singular Vessel of Devotion,
Mystical Rose,
Tower of David,
Tower of Ivory,
House of Gold,
Ark of the Covenant,
Gate of Heaven,
Morning Star,
Health of the Sick,
Refuge of Sinners,
Comforter of the Afflicted,
Help of Christians,
Queen of Angels,
Queen of Patriarchs,
Queen of Prophets,
Queen of Apostles,
Queen of Martyrs,
Queen of Confessors,
Queen of Virgins,
Queen of all Saints,
Queen conceived without Original Sin,
Queen assumed into Heaven,
Queen of the most Holy Rosary,
Queen of the Family,
Queen of Peace,
Lamb of God, Who take away the sins of the world,
   spare us, O Lord!
Lamb of God, Who take away the sins of the world,
   graciously hear us, O Lord!
Lamb of God, Who take away the sins of the world,
   have mercy on us.
V. Pray for us, O Holy Mother of God.
R. That we may be made worthy of the promises of Christ.

Let us pray: Grant, we beg Thee, O Lord God, that we Thy servants, may enjoy lasting health of mind and body, and by the glorious intercession of the Blessed Mary, ever Virgin, be delivered from present sorrow and enter into the joy of eternal happiness. Through Christ our Lord. R. Amen.

Prayer to St. Michael the Archangel

Saint Michael the Archangel, defend us in battle. Be our protection against the wickedness and snares of the devil. May God rebuke him, we humbly pray, and do thou, O prince of the heavenly hosts, by the power of God, cast into hell Satan and all the other evil spirits who prowl about the world seeking the ruin of souls. Amen.

Prayer for Priests

Almighty and Eternal God, look favorably on Christ, the Eternal and Sovereign Priest, and for love of Him, have mercy on Your priests. O most merciful God, remember that they are only weak creatures.

Constantly revive in them the grace of their ordination. Keep them close to You, lest the enemy prevail over them, so that nothing may tarnish the brilliance of their sublime vocation.

O Jesus, I pray to You for Your unfaithful and lukewarm priests, for Your priests who are beset by temptation, the enemy, and afflictions, for your sick priests, for those who will die soon, and for Your priests who are in purgatory.

Moreover, especially, I commend to You the priests who are dearest to me: the priest who baptized me, the priests who absolved me from my sins, the priests whose Masses I have attended and who have given me the Bread of Life, the priests who taught and instructed me and supported me with their help and encouragement, finally, the priests to whom I owe a special debt of thanksgiving.

O Jesus, keep them safe, close to Your Heart, and give them Your blessings abundantly, in time and eternity. Amen.

Psalm 50 (Miserere)

Have mercy on me, O God, according to Thy great mercy.

And according to the multitude of Thy tender mercies blot out my iniquity.

Wash me yet more from my iniquity, and cleanse me from my sin.

For I know my iniquity, and my sin is always before me.

To Thee only have I sinned, and have done evil before Thee: that Thou mayst be justified in Thy words and mayst overcome when Thou art judged.

For behold I was conceived in iniquities; and in sins did my mother conceive me.

For behold Thou hast loved truth: the uncertain and hidden things of Thy wisdom Thou hast made manifest to me.

Thou shalt sprinkle me with hyssop, and I shall be cleansed: Thou shalt wash me, and I shall be made whiter than snow.

To my hearing Thou shalt give joy and gladness: and the bones that have been humbled shall rejoice.

Turn away Thy face from my sins, and blot out all my iniquities.

Create a clean heart in me, O God: and renew a right spirit within my bowels.

Cast me not away from Thy face; and take not Thy Holy Spirit from me.

Restore unto me the joy of Thy salvation, and strengthen me with a perfect spirit.

I will teach the unjust Thy ways: and the wicked shall be converted to Thee.

Deliver me from blood, O God, Thou God of my salvation: and my tongue shall extol Thy justice.

O Lord, Thou wilt open my lips: and my mouth shall declare Thy praise.

For if Thou hadst desired sacrifice, I would indeed have given it: with burnt offerings Thou wilt not be delighted.

A sacrifice to God is an afflicted spirit: a contrite and humbled heart, O God, Thou wilt not despise.

Deal favourably, O Lord, in Thy good will with Sion; that the walls of Jerusalem may be built up.

Then shalt Thou accept the sacrifice of justice, oblations and whole burnt offerings: then shall they lay calves upon Thy altar.

Glory be to the Father, and to the Son, and to the Holy Ghost,

as it was in the beginning, is now, and ever shall be, world without end. Amen.

Latin Prayers

Magnificat (Canticle, Luke 1:46-55)

*Magnificat * anima mea Dominum:*

My soul doth magnify the Lord.

*et exsultavit spiritus meus * in Deo salutari meo.*

And my spirit hath rejoiced in God my Saviour.

*Quia respexit humilitatem ancillæ suæ: * ecce enim ex hoc beatam me dicent omnes generationes,*

Because He hath regarded the humility of His handmaid; for behold from henceforth all generations shall call me blessed.

*quia fecit mihi magna qui potens est: * et sanctum nomen ejus,*

Because He that is mighty, hath done great things to me; and holy is His name.

*et misericordia ejus a progenie in progenies * timentibus eum.*

And His mercy is from generation unto generations, to them that fear Him.

*Fecit potentiam in brachio suo: * dispersit superbos mente cordis sui.*

He hath shewed might in His arm: He hath scattered the proud in the conceit of their heart.

*Deposuit potentes de sede, * et exaltavit humiles.*

He hath put down the mighty from their seat, and hath exalted the humble.

*Esurientes implevit bonis: * et divites dimisit inanes.*

He hath filled the hungry with good things; and the rich He hath sent empty away.

*Suscepit Israël puerum suum, * recordatus misericordiæ suæ:*

He hath received Israel His servant, being mindful of His mercy:

*sicut locutus est ad patres nostros, * Abraham et semini ejus in sæcula*

As He spoke to our fathers, to Abraham and to his seed for ever.

*Gloria Patri et Filio, * et Spiritui Sancto,*

Glory be to the Father, and to the Son, and to the Holy Ghost,

*Sicut erat in principio, et nunc et semper, * et in saecula saeculorum. Amen.*	as it was in the beginning, is now, and ever shall be, world without end. Amen.

Salve Regina (Marian antiphon)

Salve, Regina, mater misericordiae: vita, dulcedo, et spes nostra, salve.	Hail, Holy Queen, Mother of Mercy, our life, our sweetness, and our hope.
Ad te clamamus, exsules filii Hevae.	To thee do we cry, poor banished children of Eve.
Ad te suspiramus, gementes et flentes in hac lacrimarum valle.	To thee do we send up our sighs, mourning and weeping in this valley of tears.
Eia ergo, advocata nostra, illos tuos misericordes oculos ad nos converte.	Turn then, most gracious Advocate, thine eyes of mercy towards us,
Et Jesum, benedictum fructum ventris tui, nobis post hoc exsilium ostende.	And after this our exile, show unto us the blessed fruit of thy womb, Jesus.
O clemens, o pia, o dulcis Virgo Maria!	O clement, O loving, O sweet Virgin Mary!

Anima Christi

Soul of Christ, sanctify me;
Body of Christ, save me;
Blood of Christ, inebriate me;
Water from the side of Christ, wash me;
Passion of Christ, strengthen me;
O good Jesus, hear me;
Within Your wounds, hide me;
Separated from You let me never be;
From the malignant enemy defend me;
At the hour of death call me;
And close to You bid me;
That with Your saints I may be:
Praising You for ever and ever.
Amen.

Bibliography

Sacred Scripture

- Acts: Acts of the Apostles
- Apoc: Book of the Apocalypse
- Dan: Daniel
- Gal: Epistle of Saint Paul to the Galatians
- Jn: Gospel according to Saint John
- Lk: Gospel according to Saint Luke
- Mk: Gospel according to Saint Mark
- Mt: Gospel according to Saint Matthew
- Rom: Epistle of Saint Paul to the Romans
- Tob: Book of Tobit
- I Cor: First Epistle of Saint Paul to the Corinthians
- II Cor: Second Epistle of Saint Paul to the Corinthians

Saint Alphonsus Liguori

SJJ: *La Sainteté au jour le jour* (Clovis, 2014).

Saint Anthony of Padua

Les Sermons de saint Antoine de Padoue pour l'année liturgique (Éditions franciscaines, 1944).

Saint Athanasius

See: *De Virginitate*, in *Le Muséon*, vol. XL (1927), pp. 249-264.

Saint Augustine

See: Oeuvres complètes (Vivès, 1872).

Saint Basil

Correspondance, vol. 1, *Lettres 1 à 100* (Les Belles Lettres, 2003).

Saint Bede

Opera Bedae Venerabilis (1563), Book 4, chap. 49, on Saint Luke.

Saint Benedict

PPJ: *Une pensée par jour*, compiled by Sister Véronique Dupont, O.S.B. (Médiaspaul, 2007).

Saint Bernadette

- CNI: *Le Carnet de notes intimes* (1873 and 1874), in *Les écrits de sainte Bernadette et sa voie spirituelle* (Lethielleux, 1980).
- PPJ: *Une pensée par jour*, compiled by Pascal Frey (Médiaspaul, 2012).

Saint Bernardine of Siena

Opera omnia (1745), Sermon 5 on the Nativity of the Blessed Virgin (cited also in Saint Alphonsus Liguori, *Les Gloires de Marie* [Saint Paul, 1993], 104).

Saint Catherine of Siena

- D: *Le Dialogue* (Téqui, 1976).

Charles de Foucauld

- NQ: *Notes quotidiennes*.
- PPJ: *Une pensée par jour*, compiled by Patrice Mahieu, O.S.B. (Médiaspaul, 2010).

[Curé of Ars: see St. John Vianney]

Elizabeth of the Trinity

- PPJ: *Une pensée par jour*, compiled by the Carmelites of Dijon (Médiaspaul, 2006).

Saint Francis de Sales

- IVD: *Introduction to the Devout Life* (TAN, 1994).
- PPJ: *Une pensée par jour*, compiled by Sister Marie-Christophe, Visitation Monastery, Voiron (Médiaspaul, 2008).
- XXI: "Lettres, XI," in *Oeuvres de saint François de Sales*, vol. XXI (Librairie catholique Emmanuel Vitte, 1923).

Saint Francis Xavier

- PPJ: *Une pensée par jour*, compiled by Nicolas Rousselot (Médiaspaul, 2015).

Saint Gregory Nazianzen

Discours 1-3, collection Sources chrétiennes 247 (Paris: Cerf, 1978).

Saint John Climacus
L'Échelle sainte, collection Spiritualité orientale 24 (Abbaye de Bellefontaine, 1987).

Saint John Vianney, the Curé of Ars
PPJ1: *Une pensée par jour* (Clovis, 2006).
PPJ: *Une pensée par jour*, compiled by Claudine Fearon (Médiaspaul, 2010).

Saint Justin Martyr
Apol: *Apologies* (Picard et fils, 1904).

Saint Leo the Great
Sermons I, collection Sources chrétiennes 22bis (Paris: Cerf, 1964).

Saint Louis Marie de Montfort
ASE: *Love of the Eternal Wisdom.*
VD: *True Devotion to the Blessed Virgin.*

Saint Paul of the Cross
D: *Diario spirituale* (Rome: Zoffoli, 1964).
L3: *Lettere* (Rome: A Casetti e C. Chiari, 1926).
PPJ: *Une pensée par jour*, compiled by Philippe Plet (Médiaspaul, 2011).

Pauline Jaricot
PPJ: *Une pensée par jour*, compiled by the Oeuvres Pontificales missionaires de Lyon (Médiaspaul, 2008).

Saint Peter Canisius
E: *Canisii Epistulae et acta*, vol. I (Freiburg im Breisgau: Braunsberger, 1896).

Saint Peter Julian Eymard
PPJ: *Une pensée par jour*, compiled by Sister Suzanne Aylwin (Médiaspaul, 2010).

BIBLIOGRAPHY

Padre Pio
PPJ: *Une pensée par jour*, compiled by Father Gerardo Di Flumeri, O.F.M. Cap. (Médiaspaul, 2010).

Saint Pius X
HA: *Haerens animo* (4 August 1908).

Saint Teresa of Avila
PPJ: *Une pensée par jour*, compiled by Martine Loriau (Médiaspaul, 2009).

Saint Thérèse of the Child Jesus
PPJ: *Une pensée par jour*, compiled by Hélène Mongin (Médiaspaul, 2012).

Saint Thomas Aquinas
PPJ: *Une pensée par jour*, compiled by Agnès Jauréguibéhère (Médiaspaul, 2012).

Summa theologiae.

Saint Vincent of Lerins
Commonitorium, in Nicene and Post-Nicene Fathers, Second Series, vol. 11, pp. 131-156.

Saint Vincent de Paul
PPJ: *Une pensée par jour* (Clovis, 2006).

R: *Le Rosaire, textes de saint Vincent de Paul* (Monastère de Chambarand, 2013).

Other Authors
OEC: Bossuet, *Oeuvres oratoires* vols. II and IV (Paris: Desclée de Brouwer, 1891, 1892).

365J: Father Calmel, *365 jours avec le père Calmel*, unpublished manuscript, finished in May 2014.

VF: Monseigneur Chevrot, *Les Petites Vertus du foyer* (Le Laurier, 2001).

Au. S: Léon de Clary, *L'Auréole séraphique*, vols. I and IV (Paris: Bloud et Barral, 1882).

ID: Gabriel de Sainte Marie-Madeleine, O.C.D., *Intimité divine* (Alost, Belgium: Monastery of the Discalced Carmelites, 1953).

AL: Dom Guéranger, *L'Année liturgique: le temps pascal* (TP), (H. Oudin, 1876).

Pa. S.: *Le Palmier séraphique, ou vie des saints et des hommes et femmes illustres des ordres de saint François*, vol. IV, ed. Monseigneur Paul Guérin (L. Guérin, 1872-1873).

PG: Migne, *Patrologie grecque*.

PL: Migne, *Patrologie latine*.

PS: Alain Mius, *Prier avec les saints*, vols. I, II, and III (Résiac, 2005, 2006, 2014).

FD: Saint Robert Bellarmine, quoted in Fr. Patrick Troadec, *Les Fins dernières dans les psaumes* (Clovis, 2010).

LP (Pastoral Letters)

Archbishop Gabriel de Llobet of Avignon (1933).

Bishop Théophile Louvard of Coutances et Avranches, (1947).

Bishop Octave Pasquet of Sées (1927).

Other works cited

ACP: *Ami du clergé paroissial*, vol. XVIII (Maitrier et Courtot, 1906), 367.

Bénédictins de Paris, *Vies des saints*, months of January, February, March (Letouzey et Ané, 1934, 1936. 1941).

Abbé Dunand, *Histoires choisies des Pères des déserts d'Orient* (É. Privat, 1894).

Eusebius, *Ecclesiastical History*, Book 5.

Jacques Baudouin, *Grand livre des saints* (Créer, 2006).

Pascale Moulier, *La Peinture religieuse en Haute-Auvergne* (Créer, 2007).

The Imitation of Christ.